Marx's Theory
of the Transcendence
of the State

American University Studies

Series X
Political Science

Vol. 19

PETER LANG
New York • Bern • Frankfurt am Main • Paris

John F. Sitton

Marx's Theory of the Transcendence of the State

A Reconstruction

PETER LANG
New York • Bern • Frankfurt am Main • Paris

Library of Congress Cataloging-in-Publication Data

Sitton, John F.
    Marx's theory of the transcendence of the state : a
reconstruction / John F. Sitton.
      p. cm.—(American university studies. Series X,
Political science ; vol. 19)
      Bibliography: p.
      Includes index.
      1. Marx, Karl, 1818-1883 — Contributions in political
science. 2. Communist state. I. Title. II. Series:
American university studies. Series X, Political science
; v. 19.
JC233.M299S57   1989   335.4'2—dc19   88-23390
ISBN 0-8204-0827-1   CIP
ISSN 0740-0470

CIP-Titelaufnahme der Deutschen Bibliothek

Sitton, John F.:
Marx's theory of the transcendence of the state :
a reconstruction / John F. Sitton. — New York;
Bern; Frankfurt am Main; Paris: Lang, 1989.
  (American University Studies: Ser. 10,
  Political Science; Vol. 19)
  ISBN 0-8204-0827-1

NE: American University Studies / 10

© Peter Lang Publishing, Inc., New York 1989

Printed by Weihert-Druck GmbH, Darmstadt, West Germany

For my mother and father,

Edna M. Sitton
and
William M. Sitton, Sr.

TABLE OF CONTENTS

Preface

Besides those to whom this book is dedicated, there are a number of people whose help I take great pleasure in acknowledging. Above all, Murray Levin of Boston University spent an enormous amount of time on various drafts of this work, suggesting alterations which greatly improved it. His insight into weaknesses of the argument and his sense of style made the work much clearer. This book would not have appeared without him.

I would also like to thank Howard Zinn, who originally proposed the topic. Dr. Zinn's keen comments and especially his critical imagination rescued me in my more pedantic moments.

I very much benefited from the expert technical help of John W. Miller, Information Systems and Communications Center at Indiana University of Pennsylvania, in producing the final manuscript.

There are of course equally important debts that are not academic. Among the many to whom they are owed, I would like to particularly thank Steven Rosenthal, Richard Stephen, Thomas Grilli, Earl C. Beverly, Kenneth W. Goings, and William Pearson. I'm not sure if they realize that their friendship and encouragement make all the difference.

Finally, I must thank Jacqueline Perry, Michael Lowe, Ken Lowstetter, and Deborah Luciani who in different ways have helped me understand the meaning of the words 'commitment' and 'sacrifice'. I am sure that there are other lessons down the road. When they come I hope I will be a better student.

The above debts cannot be repaid; all I can do is publicly acknowledge them. Needless to say, I have been stubborn enough to ensure that the faults of this work remain my own.

J. F. S.
June 1988

Introduction

No institution appears more critical for the existence of advanced society than the modern state. Nevertheless, Marx and Engels consistently argued that the state will be transcended as a part of the achievement of communism. From his early studies of Hegel to the *Critique of the Gotha Programme*, Marx explored the conditions necessary for the transcendence of the state. However, especially because of the historical development of socialism, this thesis is considered to be his least tenable. The theory of the transcendence of the state has been called "an incredibly naive and utopian outlook", "ideological escapism", and, by Paul Tillich, "a belief in miracles".[1] In the belief that to usefully criticize a thinker it is first necessary to know what he said, the task of this work is to reconstruct Marx's argument.

Although this theory is often referred to by Marxists and their opponents, it is perhaps the most neglected aspect of Marx's work. This neglect is accounted for, in part, by the enormous role of the state in existing socialist societies, which causes the transcendence of the state to appear to be unreasonable or at least academic for the present. Socialism necessarily entails the expansion of public decision-making and control over production, which has historically taken the form of an expansion of the activities of the state. Consequently, far from revealing any tendency to 'wither away', the state seems to be "the one indispensable institution" of socialist societies.[2]

Besides historical reasons, there are two common theoretical positions which have had the effect of marginalizing Marx's theory of the transcendence of the state. The most important is the one by which the theory is known, the 'withering away' interpretation itself. In the 'withering away' interpretation the state performs two primary functions: (1) the maintenance of the power of the economically dominant class, and (2) general management of the class antagonisms of society in order to ensure public order. With the abolition of classes by the public ownership of the means of production and with the progress of the forces of production freed of class constraints, the antagonistic character of society will disappear and the state will correspondingly lose its content much as a balloon loses its air.

In this interpretation the 'withering away' of the state is a mere concomitant of gradual changes in the economic sphere, essentially the achievement of 'abundance'. The economic sphere has an objective course of development that can be guided (somewhat) but not substantially altered by human intervention, therefore the withering away of the state is a development independent of conscious action and construction. We do not deliberate on automatic processes, therefore the transcendence of the state is not of pressing theoretical concern.

Furthermore, this process is always seen as extending into the distant future. One does not conquer scarcity in a day. In a supremely 'economic determinist' argument, the transcendence of the state is put off until adequate economic conditions have been established. Consequently, the only apparent immediate function of the theory is to distinguish Marxism from anarchism.

This predominant interpretation of the transcendence of the state as 'naturally' resulting from economic change and development is reinforced by the language in which the idea is popularly expressed. Engels' phrase "withering away" (or "dying out": *absterben*) is a metaphor taken from nature, implying an automatic or determined process. This neglects in particular the role of creation of new political forms for the transition to communism. For this reason I herein use the more appropriate (but still inadequate) phrase 'transcendence of the state'.

Another theoretical position which stands in the way of a serious analysis of the theory of the transcendence of the state is the 'instrumentalist' conception of the state. Throughout the Marxian tradition the common theory of the state is that the state is an instrument of some kind, whether wielded by a minority class (the bourgeoisie), a "caste" in the interests of a class (the aristocratic Whigs), a "band of adventurers" in the interests of a class (Locke), or even by a majority class (the proletariat).

This instrumentalist conception of the state, common to critics and Marxists alike, stems from liberal theory as developed in the classics of Hobbes, Locke, Rousseau, and James and John Stuart Mill: the state is a necessary instrument to secure certain ends which cannot be obtained by society itself. Marx and Engels themselves often promoted this view by their frequent use of terms like "machine", "engine", and "means". Quite often the only thing Marxists add to this definition of the state is the adjective 'class', that the state is an instrument utilized by one class against another.

The state *is* in certain respects an instrument. However there are two limitations to this view. First, instrumentality presupposes a unified class subject to wield it. Only in times of severe and obvious crisis does a class achieve the unity necessary for the state to be an instrument. In normal times insofar as the state is an instrument it is an instrument of class fractions and their representatives, not the class as a whole.

The second objection to instrumentalism is more fundamental. As E. B. Pashukanis argued in regard to ideology, the existence of certain structures of the capitalist mode of production is prior to their use for class ends.[3] A class does not conjure ideas from nothing; rather ideas have an objective existence (although grounded in class conditions) which precede their political use. It is not enough to show the utility of certain ideas for class purposes in order to explain them. We must also show the objective conditions which give rise to those ideas.

The same is true of the state. The state has an objective existence that is separate from and logically prior to its aspects as a class instrument and it cannot be reduced to this instrumentality. To conceive of the state as the tool of a class 'subject' obscures the real, objective relation between classes and the state. In this way this theoretical position obstructs a thorough comprehension of the theory of the transcendence of the state by: (1) making the idea of 'stateless society' a mere logical deduction from 'classless society' and (2) reducing 'classlessness' to the destruction of a 'subject', rather than the transformation of the capitalist mode of production. Many commentators have argued that there is nothing more to Marx's doctrine of the transcendence of the state than the above logical deduction: the state is a class instrument; when classes are abolished the state disappears. They then compound their mistake by not fully explaining what the 'abolition of classes' means.[4]

'Instrumentalism' and its concomitant, the 'historical subject' conception of classes, do not allow us to think through the theory of the transcendence of the state in a rigorous manner. Marx's theory analyzes the structural bases of the separation of political and social relations in the capitalist mode of production. It is this project which guides his examination of classes, the division of labor, exchange relations, and the state. His own approach leads to a much more profound view of what is entailed by the 'transcendence of the state'.

If one looks at the many formulations of Marx and Engels of the state's transcendence one is pushed beyond the simplistic and limited 'withering

4

away' interpretation. Marx conceived of the state as a structure of alienation, intimately connected with all other aspects of the capitalist mode of
production, and it is only from this standpoint that the theory can be comprehended.

One of the major historical questions for Marx, originating in
Feuerbach's study of Christianity, is how social relations of men and women
take on an independent, autonomous existence, outside their control and
constraining them.

> Individuals always proceded, and always procede, from themselves.
> Their relations are the relations of their real life process. How does
> it happen that their relations assume an independent existence over
> against them? and that the forces of their own life become superior
> to them?[5]

Marx believed this process of 'alienation' to be only one stage of human
development, that a society is possible in which the relations which spring
from social interaction are subject to common control. This belief is firmly expressed in the only area he analyzed systematically, i.e. capitalist
production, but it is also present in other aspects of his work, e.g. the production of ideas and in the political realm. The state is one of the manifestations
of alienation and can be transcended as a part of the process of abolishing
the bases of alienation.

This orientation is superior to the 'withering away' thesis in many
respects. It indicates that the goal is *not* the disappearance of a set of functions (e.g. coercion) which belong to the state but a "reabsorption" (to use
Marx's phrase) of these functions by society. The issue of the 'withering
away' of the functions of the state has led to many fruitless arguments.
Rather the formulation of 'alienation' asks not whether certain functions
can disappear but whether they need be performed by an independent institution. This is not to deny that the disappearance of some functions is a
part of the theory of the transcendence of the state but that this is misleading if taken as the *predominant* concern. 'Absorption', not abolition, of
functions is much more interesting and reasonable a possibility.

Secondly, regarding the state as a kind of alienation emphasizes the ob-
jective-structural aspect of the state as an institution. It focuses the argument on the generation and maintenance of *objective* processes which cul-
minate in the state as a separate sphere in a larger whole. This allows us to

view the state and its transcendence in the broad context of the abolition of the processes of alienation. Henri Lefebvre sees the transcendence of the state in precisely these terms, quite reminiscent of the early Marx:

> Human unity, dissociated at the individual, social, economic, and political levels, will be restored only when society as a whole, transformed by revolutionary action, has absorbed the state, organized economic life, and enabled the individual to reconstruct himself on new foundations, without legal systems or other external constraints.[6]

This viewpoint has been echoed by Istvan Meszaros and, in criticism of existing socialism, by Adam Schaff.[7]

The alienation interpretation thereby avoids the subjectivist view of the state as an instrument of classes conceived as unified, historical subjects. As I will argue, one of the major reasons for the state's existence is precisely to *constitute* the bourgeoisie as an historical actor. This cannot be comprehended by any of the popular instrumentalist interpretations which are inspired, of course, by certain phrases of Marx himself.

Finally, the alienation approach is superior to the 'withering away' interpretation in that it conceives communism not as the creation of a harmonious productive process established by the abolition of classes but as the creation of a system of production which structurally ensures *collective control*. 'Control', not 'harmony', is the definition of communism. Expectations of instituting a naturally harmonious process of production are nothing more than hopes of fulfilling the dream of liberalism. Power, not harmony, is the primary question of communism, as it is of all human societies. Socialist theory has been distracted far too long by the chimera of harmony.

For all its usefulness, there is at least one major danger in conceiving the state as a kind of 'alienation', a danger that Marx did not always successfully avoid. In utilizing the concept 'alienation' in social theory there is a tendency for 'society' to become the sole causal factor, with politics and ideas taking on the role of 'appearance' to an 'essence'. Politics and ideas become mere "expressions" (Marx's frequent term) of something else, depriving political and ideological *structures* of all independent efficacy.

In the late 1880s and early 1890s Engels repeatedly cautioned against depriving ideology and the state of independent importance for determining social activity and change.

6

Marx and I are ourselves partly to blame for the fact that the younger people sometimes lay more stress on the economic side than is due it. We had to emphasize the main principle *vis-a-vis* our adversaries, who denied it, and we had not always the time, the place or the opportunity to give their due to the other factors involved in the interaction.[8]

Against the tendency to minimize the efficacy of these structures, regardless of one's view of their origin, we must insist that ideological and political structures are *real*, that is that they have an independent effect on social activity.

The reduction of the political to mere alienated "expression" of something else is one of the reasons for the undervaluation in Marx's work of the importance of political structures and for the impoverishment of Marxian political theory. This underdevelopment has been noted by, among others, Lucio Colletti:

The development of political theory has been extraordinarily weak in Marxism. ...both Marx and Lenin envisaged the transition to socialism and the realization of communism on a world scale as an extremely swift and proximate process. The result was that the sphere of political structures remained little examined or explored. One could formulate this paradoxically by saying that the political movement inspired by Marxism has been virtually innocent of political theory.[9]

The concept 'alienation' need not contribute to this "innocence", as Marx proved by taking alienated labor as the basis of capitalist production and showing how the objectifications of social interaction can take on an autonomous and oppressive form. However it is not enough to simply indicate the bases of political alienation, as the 'expression' variant does. We must also examine the specific structures of the political as an alienated sphere and how these specific structures interact with and help maintain the bases of alienation. As I hope to establish in the following pages, this was essentially the approach of Marx and is the only way in which we can explicate and evaluate his theory of the transcendence of the state.

To forestall an immediate objection, it is necessary to raise here the possibility that Marx and Engels had differing notions of the transcendence of the state. Shlomo Avineri, for example, has argued that there is a different use of terms by Marx and Engels on the topic which indicates a substantial difference in their conceptions in this regard.[10] According to Avineri, Marx expressed the idea with the word "aufhebung" rather than Engels' "absterben". 'Aufhebung' has a specific philosophical meaning of overcoming two poles of an opposition and 'preserving' them in a 'higher' unity. 'Absterben', as previously noted, implied the disappearance of one term of the opposition, leaving the other, the 'economic', substantially unchanged.[11] Avineri believes that Marx and Engels were at odds over the meaning of the transcendence of the state and that it shows in their respective terminology.

Richard Adamiak has (unintentionally) provided additional evidence for the possibility of a distinction between Marx and Engels on the issue by pointing out that the celebrated passage in *Anti-Duehring* in which the phrase 'withering away' occurs only appeared in the second edition, after Marx's death.[12] If Marx had had an objection to the implications of this phrase he could not respond.

It is clear that the phrase 'withering away' is misleading if meant to convey the complete theory of the state's transcendence, whatever its merits for bringing out certain aspects of this process. However we cannot use this phrase to drive a wedge between Marx and Engels on the issue. Although Avineri is correct that 'aufhebung' better expresses the theory, Engels' 'absterben' is no more than an ill-considered choice of words upon which too much attention has been focused. To the best of my knowledge, 'withering away' only occurs twice in Engels' work: in the later editions of *Anti-Duehring* and in *Socialism: Utopian and Scientific*. Since the latter pamphlet is composed of sections of *Anti-Duehring*, essentially 'withering away' only occurs *once*.[13]

As will be clear from my citations, Marx and Engels used many phrases to express the idea of the transcendence of the state.[14] Marx often used terms similar to 'withering away' and Engels fully appreciated other aspects of the theory that cannot be comprehended by the word 'absterben'. It is unfortunate that the theory has become known by this limited term.

Another argument against Avineri's attempt to distinguish Marx and Engels on this issue is that the term 'aufhebung' does not necessarily mean, even in Marx's work, abolition and preservation, i.e. what it means in

Hegelian philosophy. 'Aufhebung' is frequently used by Marx to mean simply 'abolition', which is a quite proper German usage.

Avineri engages in what Michael Evans has called "a favorite game nowadays ... to separate Marx from Engels."[15] Although I reserve judgment on other issues, there seems to be no substantial distinction between Marx and Engels on the transcendence of the state. The only difference is Engels rather intemperate use of broad historical generalizations. This gift of generalization and memorable phrases ("withers away") served Engels well as the first popularizer of Marxism but could have misled the first generations of Marxists for whom Engels' work was much more accessible than that of Marx. An understanding of the theory of the transcendence of the state can only be reached by examining the whole of Marx and Engels' work, much of which was not even published until long after the first generation had formed its opinions.

Considering the relative neglect of Marx's theory of the transcendence of the state, the present work is primarily one of reconstruction. After briefly exploring certain arguments of Saint-Simon which probably suggested the idea to Marx, in the first part I explore the development of Marx's theory of the transcendence of the state in his early works. Special attention is paid to Marx's critique of Hegel's political philosophy because this contains the first formulation of the theory. In this critique Marx presented several themes which oriented his discussion of the issue throughout his life. Hopefully my examination of Marx's critique of Hegel will help clarify some of the particularly obscure passages of the only work explicitly on political philosophy that Marx produced.

In other works Marx explored the *simultaneous* creation of the capitalist economy and the modern state. Marx's theory of the transcendence of the state is historically specific: capitalist social relations and modern political relations are parts of an internally differentiated totality. In these works Marx concentrated mainly on the fragmenting effects of the exchange relations of capitalism which entail an independent institutional embodiment of community, i.e. a "representative" of society, the modern state. In *The German Ideology*, however, Marx and Engels turned their attention to the structure of capitalist *production*, in particular to the division of labor. Although the concept 'division of labor' allows Marx and Engels to further develop their theory of the conditions under which the state would no longer be necessary, the concept is actually too broad to fully explicate the relation between the capitalist productive system as a whole and the modern state. Therefore after reconstructing their arguments about the division of labor, in two successive chapters (one on production, the other on exchange) I pursue Marx's more detailed discussion.

Having established the relation of capitalist production and exchange to the state, it is then possible to turn to the actual political arguments Marx and Engels made specifically on the transcendence of the state. There are three different formulations of the theory but I believe that they can be reconciled by examining the important emphasis of Marx on the nature of the transitional regime, especially his analysis of the "revolution against the state", the Paris Commune of 1871. This enables us to see the theory as a whole.

Finally, I attempt to briefly evaluate Marx's project of the development of stateless society by a critique of two key points of his doctrine: (1) his argument concerning proletarian political representation and (2) certain difficulties of the possibility of the abolition of the division of labor. In a work of this kind, immanent critique seems more useful and appropriate than the alternatives.

As this is a work of reconstruction of an important topic of Marx, it is necessary to engage in a considerable amount of exegesis. This is unavoidable. Also unavoidable is the level of abstraction at which Marx's argument unfolds. The abstract character of the theory of the transcendence of the state may diminish its persuasiveness. However I believe that it was the only manner in which Marx could express the truth that political relations are historically specific, and therefore historically alterable.

1. Respectively: Henry B. Mayo, *Introduction to Marxist Theory* (New York: Oxford University Press, 1960), p. 172; Ghita Ionescu, "Introduction" to *The Political Thought of Saint-Simon*, edited by Ionescu (London: Oxford University Press, 1976), p. 11; Paul Tillich, *The Socialist Decision* (New York: Harper and Row, Publishers, 1977), p. 76.

2. Richard Adamiak, "The 'Withering Away of the State': A Reconsideration," *The Journal of Politics* Volume 32, Number 1 (February 1970), p. 17.

3. Evgeny B. Pashukanis, *Law and Marxism: A General Theory* [1924] (London: Ink Links, 1978), p. 140.

4. Mayo, *Marxist Theory*, pp. 164-166. A more sophisticated view that reaches the same conclusions is G.D.H. Cole, *The Meaning of Marxism* (Ann Arbor: University of Michigan Press, 1966), p. 182.

5. Karl Marx and Frederick Engels, "The German Ideology," in *Collected Works* Volume 5 (New York: International Publishers, 1976), p. 93.

6. Henri Lefebvre, *The Sociology of Marx* (New York: Vintage Books, 1969), p. 125.

7. Istvan Meszaros, *Marx's Theory of Alienation* (London: Merlin Press, 1970), pp. 129-130; Adam Schaff, *Marxism and the Human Individual* (New York: McGraw-Hill Book Company, 1970), p. 128 and p. 138.

8. Engels, letter to Joseph Bloch (September 21, 1890), in *Marx-Engels Selected Correspondence* (Moscow: Progess Publishers, 1975), p. 396.

9. "Lucio Colletti: A Political and Philosophical Interview," by Perry Anderson, in *Western Marxism: A Critical Reader* (London: New Left Books, 1977), p. 331.

10. Shlomo Avineri, *The Social and Political Thought of Karl Marx* (London: Cambridge University Press, 1968), pp. 202-203.

11. Ibid., p. 203.

12. Adamiak, "The 'Withering Away of the State'," p. 16.

13. It is quite possible that the phrase was originally in *Socialism: Utopian and Scientific* (published in 1880) and therefore that Marx was aware of it. Engels explained in his preface to the second edition of *Anti-Duehring* (New York: International Publishers, 1976) that he took some phrases for that edition from the above popular tract: p. 14.

14. See also Hal Draper, "The Death of the State in Marx and Engels," *The Socialist Register 1970*, edited by Ralph Miliband and John Saville (London: Merlin Press, 1970), p. 281; also Michael Evans, "Marx Studies," *Political Studies* Volume XVIII, Number 4 (December 1970), pp. 528-535.

15. Evans, "Marx Studies," p. 531.

Chapter 1

The Vision of Saint-Simon

In April of 1883 Engels wrote a letter in the course of which he summarized the idea of the transcendence of the state:

> Marx and I, ever since 1845, have held the view that one of the results of the future proletarian revolution will be the gradual dissolution and ultimate disappearance of that political organization called *the state*; an organization the main object of which is to secure, by armed force, the economical subjection of the working majority to the wealthy minority. With the disappearance of a wealthy minority the necessity for an armed, repressive state-force disappears also.[1]

Engels was correct that this idea was a long-held concern of theirs, and it is true that it was not related to *proletarian* revolution until around 1845. However Marx's discussion of the transcendence of the state precedes 1845 and is one of the most enduring topics in his work.

As is universally acknowledged, Marx's notion of the transcendence of the state originated in the work of Saint-Simon. However, the exact relation between Saint-Simon's political perspective and the ideas of Marx has been rarely explored.[2] Therefore it is important at the outset to provide a very brief review of Saint-Simon's political ideas, indicating their probable influence on Marx. It is not my purpose to critique Saint-Simon, only to select arguments that influenced Marx's own conception.

Saint-Simon had an important impact on the 'Young Hegelians' with whom the youthful Marx associated. As Z. A. Jordan reports,

> The conceptual similarity between the Saint-Simonists and the Young Hegelians is considerable and prompted a contemporary scholar to describe the doctrine of the latter as 'Hegelized Saint-Simonism'.[3]

The similarity lies in Saint-Simon's belief that all political, social, and religious institutions rest on ideas and that it is impossible to create a new social system without (1) criticism of the ideas on which the old rests and (2) elaboration of the philosophical foundation of the new.

Although Marx was later to violently attack this conception of the role of ideas, his and Engels' reception of Saint-Simon's work was by no means a passing fancy. In *The Manifesto of the Communist Party* they referred to the "originators of these systems" -- the utopian communists Fourier, Owen, and Saint-Simon -- as "in many respects revolutionary". They reserved their severe criticism for the disciples of the utopians who had formed quasi-religious sects.[4] In particular Marx and Engels mentioned the notion of "the conversion of the functions of the state into a mere superintendence of production" as a valuable idea, although purely utopian unless combined with a theory of the abolition of class antagonisms.[5]

Much later, in *Anti-Duehring*, Engels again commented on Saint-Simon's political conceptions, concluding:

> In Saint-Simon we find the breadth of a genius, thanks to which almost all the ideas of later socialists which are not strictly economic are contained in his works in embryo.[6]

Ignoring the polemical exaggeration, this is still a ringing endorsement and it is obvious that we should uncover why Marx and Engels were so fond of Saint-Simon's political ideas, especially in regard to the transcendence of the state.

There are several arguments of Saint-Simon which are relevant to this topic: (1) that the interdependence of industrial society engenders a unity of purpose; (2) that 'politics' is thereby transformed, i.e. the nature of authority changes; and (3) that this is the inauguration of the rule of knowledge.

According to Saint-Simon, the nature of politics is necessarily altered with the passage from a "militaristic" (feudal) society to an industrial society. Like many of his contemporaries, Saint-Simon believed that feudalism was based on "plunder", whereas industrial society is based on cooperative production.[7] The major characteristic of feudalism was war and the division of society into rulers and ruled. In sharp contrast the chief characteristic of industrial society is interdependence of all sectors of production, yielding a 'unity of purpose'.

This necessarily leads to a change in the "technique" of politics.[8] With the passage from pre-industrial society to industrial society the "politics of power" is replaced by a "politics without power" (Ghita Ionescu's phrase) or a "politics of ability" (Saint-Simon). Assuming a unity of purpose resulting from interdependent production, the sole issue in industrial society is the best arrangement of the various productive abilities of its members. Ghita Ionescu sums up Saint-Simon's argument in this fashion:

> Thus the political process of command-obedience, which had proved increasingly unworkable in the new conditions, is replaced by the process of persuasion-understanding.[9]

Saint-Simon expected that those with more knowledge would have greater powers of persuasion, therefore the new society would be more or less meritocratic.

This proposed power of those with knowledge is the basis of the common interpretation of Saint-Simon as a technocratic elitist. However this interpretation overlooks the fact that although in Saint-Simon's conception the knowledgeable 'rule', they do not rule in the usual sense of having recourse to coercion. The unity of purpose implicit in interdependent production makes coercion superfluous. Instead of politics being a struggle for instruments of power, as in feudalism, in industrial society

> politics is the science of production -- that is to say, that science whose object is the creation of an order of things most favorable to every kind of production.[10]

For Saint-Simon, as for Aristotle, politics is the 'master art'.

In this way Saint-Simon envisioned the realization of an age-old dream: authority based on knowledge, not coercion. In his excellent commentary on Saint-Simon, Emile Durkheim identified Saint-Simon's projected society with anarchism:

> As its authority stems not from the fact that it is the strongest but because it knows what others are ignorant of, its action will have nothing arbitrary or coercive about it. It will not do merely what it wishes, but what fits the nature of things, and as no one wants to act other than in conformity with the nature of things, one will do as it says without having to compel it. One will voluntarily follow its directions, just as the sick man follows his physician's, the engineer that of the chemist and mathematician, the worker that of the engineer.[11]

Since 'government' properly so-called (i.e. "imperative authority") is unnecessary, industrial society is "anarchistic".[12] In Saint-Simon's words, 'government' is replaced by "functional administration".[13]

If one accepts Saint-Simon's major assumption of a unity of purpose emerging from the interdependence of industrial society, it is clear that this transformation of the nature of authority is possible. Why it is *necessary* is another question entirely. Ionescu has developed an argument as to its necessity which he presents as Saint-Simon's own. Although it is very difficult to find this argument in Saint-Simon's work,[14] it is an interesting elaboration and not only makes Saint-Simon more persuasive but is also quite relevant to Marx's theory of the transcendence of the state. (Ionescu himself thinks that there is little in Marx's doctrine that is worth repeating.)

According to Ionescu, the interdependence of industrial society necessarily ensures a 'unity of purpose' because it produces a diffusion of power throughout the economic system.

> So interdependent are the elements of society and yet, on the contrary, all those who produce goods and deliver services have become so independent in that society, through their own expertise, that the withholding of services or of production by any of these innumerable groups of industrialists can immediately stop the functioning of the entire society. Power is nowhere because power is everywhere.[15]

In industrial society anyone who performs a service or has an ability necessary to the functioning of society has power; power is no longer concentrated in a particular stratum, e.g. the nobility.

The consequence of this diffusion of power is clear: all who participate in production by using their skills and knowledge must also be allowed to participate in decision-making.[16] "Lack of consultation becomes in a literal sense dysfunctional and leads to breakdown."[17] It is this diffusion of power that protects society against technocracy and creates the unbiased rule by the knowledgeable. Coercion is not only unnecessary in industrial society, because of the unity of purpose in increasing production, but structurally *impossible* because of interdependence and the ability of any group to withdraw its services. There is a minority veto on all public policy.

If we accept Ionescu's interpretation of Saint-Simon's theory, we see three elements which transform the nature of authority in industrial society: (1) extreme interdependence of all sectors of production, (2) unity of purpose produced by this interdependence, and (3) the ability of any group in society to stop the functioning of the whole, i.e. a diffusion of power resulting from interdependence. Having outlined Saint-Simon's theory of industrial society we can give a few general criticisms of his theory and then see how his ideas are related to Marx's conception of the transcendence of the state.

There are several immediate objections to Saint-Simon's theory of politics in industrial societies. First, although it is true that interdependence characterizes industrial society, interdependence does not necessarily lead to a unity of purpose, at least not in the way that Saint-Simon imagined. It is the division of labor that establishes interdependence and the division of labor has contrary tendencies. It *can* serve as the source of unity through the consciousness of the agents in the productive process of the necessity of coordinated action. However it can also produce extreme fragmentation of a society, each pursuing the immediate interests which result from her or his particular position in the division of labor, without concern for other positions and their interests. From the division of labor alone as a starting point one can prove nothing. It is necessary to explicate how the different positions in the division of labor are coordinated: through a market, through an all-powerful central apparatus, through a religious belief system, or some other way. Unless these other aspects are delineated one begs the question of 'unity of purpose'.

One of the most frequent objections to anti-state arguments is precisely that the division of labor is inherently frag- menting, that the interdependence of industrial society *necessitates* a strong state. These critics believe that advanced society would not be able to function with the possibility of a minority veto by production groups. From the same evidence they draw a conclusion exactly the opposite of Saint-Simon.

A completely different problem with Saint-Simon's theory concerns the proposed rule of knowledge. First, the identification of knowledge and persuasiveness is false. As Plato pointed out long ago in *The Gorgias*, knowledge and persuasiveness are very different things. Saint-Simon did not adequately define a situation in which they could become identical; it remains on the level of assertion.

Secondly, to rule "in accordance with the nature of things" (Durkheim's phrase) depends upon clearly identifying exactly what the 'nature of things' *is* to the satisfaction of all concerned. In most cases conflict is not only possible but even necessary to determining what actually is the 'nature of things'. The truth cannot be arrived at in one leap, at least by most people,

18

but rather is a series of approximations, clarified by discussion. Saint-Simon's theory does not contribute to an answer to this ancient problem.

Finally, there is a third kind of objection to the smooth course supposedly inaugurated by the rule of knowledge. In many cases in determining the 'best course' we are comparing apples and oranges. There are many 'goods', not one, and public policy is at best a compromise between different 'goods'. For example, the most benevolent socialist society would have to confront questions like 'more productive machines or humanization of the workplace?', and 'longer workweek for more production or greater leisure time?'. Presumably majority rule would decide, but majority rule undermines the basis of the 'minority veto' on which Ionescu, in elaborating Saint-Simon's doctrine, pinned his hopes.

Many of these criticisms apply to other proponents of stateless society, including Marx. Marx's theory must be partly evaluated by how well he produces answers to these problems.

Two of Saint-Simon's ideas found a clear expression in Marx's own theory. First, Marx's vision of the final role of decision-making institutions is similar to Saint-Simon's. Saint-Simon imagined the actual institutional form of the new politics as the "administrative council of the great industrial company formed by the whole society."[18] He expected the development of a vast network of industrial associations, superceding the nation-states of Europe. At first the new industrial groups will exist alongside the present governments, which will exercise their traditional role of coercion against criminals, but as the new order developed the latter bodies will become unimportant.[19] People will find their place in society and be able to share in the increasing production. The administrative council would not (and, according to Ionescu, *could* not) 'stand apart' from and in a superior relation to other social structures; it will merely form another branch of the division of labor.[20]

This idea of government being reduced to an undistinguished role in the division of labor, not standing apart in a separate and superior relation to society, is a crucial aspect of Marx's conception of the transcendence of the state and is expressed throughout his work. Its exact meaning is unclear but it is certain that Marx's notion originated in Saint-Simon's vision.

The second aspect of Saint-Simon's theory which influenced Marx's own is the assertion that the interdependence of industrial society results in a 'unity of purpose'. Overall Marx and Engels assumed that the abolition of classes by the common ownership of the means of production would eliminate any fundamental disagreement over broad policy alternatives in the new society. Furthermore, in a way Marx agreed with Saint-Simon/Ionescu that a unity of purpose *necessarily* emerges because the modern productive process can only be operated jointly. In many places Marx asserted that the modern means of production can only be utilized in common, although he never explained exactly why this is so. Exploring his possible reasoning on this matter will be a major aspect of later chapters of this work.

However Marx could never have been satisfied with Saint-Simon's arguments for the development of a unity of purpose; he had additional reasons for its emergence. For Marx the historical development of the proletariat and the revolutionary process itself create some basis for unity in post-revolutionary society. The establishment of direct democracy on the model of the Paris Commune of 1871 would also ensure the transformation of government into just another branch of the division of labor. Further exploration of these topics here would presuppose much of my later analysis but the connection between certain theses of Saint-Simon and Marx is clear.

There is a specifically Marxian criticism to be made of Saint-Simon. Saint-Simon, like his contemporaries (e.g. James Mill), believed the 'industrialists' to be the natural champions of the proletariat. Both groups comprised the Third Estate and Saint-Simon usually used the word "industrialist" to mean both.

Marx and Engels frequently characterized utopian socialism as the expression of proletarian aspirations before sharp class struggle developed. As they saw it, when the Third Estate became victorious, its internal antagonisms showed themselves and the unity of purpose upon which Saint-Simon's theory rested was destroyed. Any utilization of Saint-Simon's insights would have to relate them to the society organized *after* the triumph of the proletariat, which is precisely their role in Marx's thought.

The above criticisms aside, there are several ideas of Saint-Simon which go directly to the heart of the discussion of the transcendence of the state. First, the notion that the nature of authority will change in classless society is a central theme of commentary on Marx's theory. It is the possibility of a different kind of authority that serves as the basis for arguments about the disappearance of law.

Secondly, as mentioned before, the idea that the governing body need not stand in a "representative relation" to society (Marx's term), that in some manner it can form an undistinguished branch of the division of labor, is the central conception which guides all of Marx's theorizing of the transcendence of the state, from his critique of Hegel to his most mature works.

Finally, Saint-Simon's argument that industrial society produces a tendency to the diffusion of power has some truth. It is a major strategy of capitalists to fight this tendency by removing all power over the productive process from the shop floor. There are several ways of doing this: sharply separating tasks requiring knowledge from those of execution, reducing the need for skilled labor, increasing the use of machines, etc. The tendency toward a diffusion of power is a major characteristic of industrial societies although Saint-Simon did not foresee the possibility of combatting it nor the transformation of the labor-process which would occur in order to do so.

To conclude, Saint-Simon expressed many ideas which provoked Marx's thought on the possibility of stateless society. There is good reason why Marx and Engels found Saint-Simon so suggestive. However, Saint-Simon's ideas are only a sketch of the problems and his Enlightenment optimism vitiates some of his analysis. Furthermore there is a central issue that Saint-Simon did not explore and, as Marx suggested, *could* not explore: the existence of classes. As Marx stated repeatedly, the abolition of classes is always the key to any serious discussion of the possibility of transcending the state.

1. Frederick Engels, letter to van Patten (April 18, 1883), in *Marx-Engels Selected Correspondence* (Moscow: Progress Publishers, 1975), p. 340.

2. Z. A. Jordan, "Introduction" to *Karl Marx: Economy, Class, and Social Revolution*, edited by Jordan (London: Thomas Nelson and Sons, Ltd., 1971). Jordan is the rare and valuable exception to the rule.

3. Ibid., p. 35, footnote.

4. "The Manifesto of the Communist Party," in *The Revolutions of 1848: Political Writings Volume I*, edited and introduced by David Fernbach (New York: Random House, 1974), p. 96.

5. Ibid., p. 96.

6. Frederick Engels, *Herr Eugen Duehring's Revolution in Science* [*Anti-Duehring*] (New York: International Publishers, 1976), p. 284.

7. Jordan, "Introduction," p. 31.

8. Ghita Ionescu, "Introduction" to *The Political Thought of Saint-Simon*, edited by Ionescu (London: Oxford University Press, 1976), p. 11.

9. Ionescu, "Introduction," p. 39.

10. Saint-Simon in ibid., p. 108.

11. Emile Durkheim, *Socialism and Saint-Simon* (Yellow Springs, OH.: The Antioch Press, 1958), pp. 154-155.

12. Ibid., pp. 154-155.

13. Ionescu, "Introduction," p. 42.

14. Ibid., pp. 35-40. There is no mention of this in the appropriate place by Durkheim: see *Socialism*, pp. 138-139.

15. Ionescu, "Introduction," p. 35.

16. Ibid., p. 39.

17. Ibid., p. 40.

18. Durkheim, *Socialism*, pp. 154-155; see also Ionescu, p. 42.

19. Durkheim, *Socialism*, p. 152.

20. "It will not be above those it directs, but will simply have another role." Durkheim, *Socialism*, pp. 154-155.

Chapter 2

The Initial Formulation: Marx's Critique of Hegel

Marx first raised the possibility of the transcendence of the state in his *A Contribution to the Critique of Hegel's Philosophy of Right*. Although still relatively neglected, this is the only work by Marx on political philosophy and is of great importance for understanding his conception of the state. Marx developed a perspective in the *Critique* which, although enriched by later analysis, he never abandoned.[1]

The *Critique* presents several immediate problems of interpretation, containing broad generalizations and close textual criticism, political points and purely philosophical discussion, all jumbled together. The scope is so broad and disorderly that the book never satisfactorily completes many essential arguments. The greatest difficulty, however, is Marx's terminology. There is the usual unclarity of the language of German idealism but the problem is more specific than that. In particular Marx used the words 'state' and 'democracy' in ways that must be clearly grasped in order to follow his reasoning.

In ordinary political discourse the word 'state' is used in at least two ways: to indicate a nation as a whole (e.g. the 'state of Mexico') *and* to refer specifically to the governing apparatus of a nation. The former is of course the more inclusive. In this early work Marx had to struggle with a similar dualistic usage. Correspondingly, in the *Critique* Marx used the word 'state' to mean 'true community', a community in which the 'essence' of man (free, conscious association) coincides with his existence. He used the phrase 'political state' or 'constitution' to refer simply to the governing apparatus.

Marx's usage is a response to Hegel. Hegel made no such distinction in his uses of the word 'state'. By 'state' he meant the concept of a free, conscious community *and* the institutional forms through which this community is realized. Infrequently Hegel spoke of this "actualization of the concept through its self-differentiation" as the "constitution" and in only three places as the "strictly political state".[2] This is justified in Hegel's philosophy in which concepts do not stand apart from the world but actualize themselves in it. However it leads to confusion and much of Marx's critique is an attempt to distinguish these two meanings and aspects of the state.

Marx clarified their relation in this way: 'state' is community; it either exists or its does not. The 'political state' or apparatus is charged with creating the 'state'. Marx's general conclusion against Hegel is that the 'political state' *by its very mode of existence* is incapable of creating the 'state'.

These introductory comments are necessary because some commentators have interpreted Marx as having dropped the broad meaning of the 'state' in his later works.[3] This is untrue. Throughout Marx's work the word 'state' always retained the sense of an 'arena of universality'; it was never simply reduced to 'the governing apparatus', as instrumentalist versions would have it. The importance of the dual sense of the word 'state' will become clear as we examine his other works. Furthermore it is necessary to keep in mind the above remarks in order to understand the initial formulation of the transcendence of the state, as well as to comprehend Marx's peculiar and extremely important use of the term 'democracy' in his critique of Hegel's political theory.

In this critique Marx originated many themes of his later work. It is unnecessary to produce a general evaluation of Marx's arguments against Hegel; I will concentrate on the specific topics which are relevant to the theory of the transcendence of the state. First, however, it is necessary to engage in a brief overview of Hegel's political philosophy.

Hegel wished to show how the elements of modern states lead to the realization of free, conscious, ethical community, the actualization of "objective spirit". His theory was a response to the liberal theories of Hobbes, Locke, and Rousseau. Hegel clearly perceived the aspects of capitalism which obstruct the realization of community: the fragmenting effects of the division of labor, problems of commodity production, and the general inadequacy of market forces for producing prosperity. Shlomo Avineri did not exaggerate when he called Hegel "one of the earliest radical critics of the modern industrial system."[4]

For Hegel, however, the role of philosophy is to interpret the world, not change it. Unlike Marx, Hegel tried to integrate the sphere of 'egoism', the "system of needs"[5] (i.e. capitalism), into the 'state'.[6] That which exists has a rational core and must be integrated into a whole, not in every detail but in its main principle. Of course Hegel's philosophy is no more completely quiescent than Marx's early work is completely voluntaristic. The difference between the two can be summed up in this way: for Hegel, that which exists is expressive of "Reason"; for Marx, that which exists, exists for 'reasons', historically limited in their validity. For Hegel, therefore, capitalism must become one moment in a totality.

Hegel attempted to integrate the "system of needs" into the state by a series of institutions which would mediate the contradiction between the 'particularity' of civil society and the 'universality' of objective Spirit. These institutions, the "Corporations" and the "Estates", will be examined shortly.

Marx's central point against Hegel is simply that his mediations do not work. At best Hegel's 'Estates' merely reintroduce the problems of civil society on the political level. (It is even possible that Hegel's political program would tend to *increase* the problems of civil society.) The concrete institutional measures by which the state is supposed to actualize itself, i.e. the "strictly political state" or "constitution", are external to civil society, confronting it as a coercive force. The state as the actualization of freedom and universality remains opposed to civil society; the 'state' only exists as an abstract ideal.

According to Marx, Hegel's political apparatus does not universalize civil society and one of the *proofs* of this is the very existence of the political apparatus separate from society. (Another proof is that Hegel's 'state' only really exists, by his own admission, in "times of exigency".)[7] Marx believed that a true community (a 'state') can only be developed directly from civil society, not from above. He concluded that the creation of a 'state' would completely alter the relation of the governing apparatus to society. This apparatus would no longer stand in a separate and superior relation (i.e. a "representative relation") to the rest of society. When true community is developed the primary distinction between state and society will simply collapse. In his work on Hegel's political philosophy Marx not only rejected Hegel's political mediations, he rejected *all* political mediations.

Marx's entire argument against Hegel's mediating political institutions takes the form of a criticism of the separation of 'political state' and 'civil society' which the problem of mediation presupposes. Three aspects of Marx's critique are essential to understanding the later development of the idea of the transcendence of the state. These are (1) his discussion of the Estates system, (2) his analysis of 'representation', and (3) his prescription of 'universal suffrage' and the particular conception of democracy which supports it.

In Hegel's formulation, the Estates play the key role in mediating civil society and the state. Of the two Estates, one exists for the business class and the other for landed property. The business Estate forms the lower house of the legislature. The 'system of needs' has already been partly elevated from its particularity by the formation of "corporations", groups established on the level of civil society for the furtherance and regulation of limited interests (e.g. each major trade, scholastic bodies, etc. would have its 'corporation').[8] In contrast, the landed Estate forms the upper house of the legislature.

In this way the real distinctions in civil society between capitalist property and landed property and the modes of life that arise with them achieve separate political expression. For Hegel, enduring divisions in civil society should not be ignored on the political level but rather must be given separate institutional form. Step by step, the particularity of civil society is mediated into the universality of the state. Contrary to liberal political theory, there should be no sharp break between civil and political life.

> The circles of association of civil society are already communities. To picture these communities as once more breaking up into a mere conglomeration of individuals as soon as they enter into the field of politics, i.e. the field of the highest concrete universality, is *eo ipso* to hold civil and political life apart from one another and as it were to hang the latter in the air ...[9]

The Estates give these existing communities expression on a higher level.

The Estates are aided in their task by the "universal class", the bureaucracy of the executive branch, selected by merit, not by social class. The role of the bureaucracy is to subsume particular cases which arise in civil society under general principles. The impartiality of the bureaucracy is established by making the individual bureaucrat's livelihood entirely dependent on the state. (Needless to say, this is one of Hegel's weakest arguments.)

Therefore in Hegel's conception there are four mediating institutions which raise civil society out of its particularity: (1) the corporations which create limited groups around particular interests on the level of civil society (which only bears on the business Estate), (2) the business Estate constituted of representatives of the corporations (those preconstituted 'communities') which forms the lower house, (3) the landed Estate which forms the upper house, and (4) the universal class, the bureaucracy.

Hegel's institutions of 'corporations' and 'Estates' are obviously modelled on the institutions of medieval society. 'Corporations' are very similar to guilds, trading associations, monastic orders, and other closed groups. The Estates were the political expression of social classes or, more precisely, they were simultaneously political and class entities. Estates were real communities, separated by different modes of life and different privileges. For this reason, according to Marx, the medieval state was completely different from the modern state. It was more an alliance of Estates held together by nationality.

> Their class was their state. The relationship of the various states to the Empire was one of transactions at the level of *nationality*; for the political state, as distinct from civil society, was nothing but the *representation of nationality*.[10]

Estates did not have to be *given* political significance by incorporation into the political sphere because they were at once political and social.[11]

Marx argued that Hegel's attempt to raise class distinctions to political significance by a resurrected Estates system is based on his failure to understand the essential difference between 'Estates' and modern class distinctions.

> In the Middle Ages there were serfs, feudal property, trade guilds, scholastic corporations, etc. That is to say, in the Middle Ages property, trade, society, and man were *political*; the material content of the state was defined by its form; every sphere of private activity had a political character, or was a political sphere; in other words politics was characteristic of the different spheres of private life.[12]

Modern society is distinguished precisely by the privatization of property and social activities. The destruction of feudal obligations and regulations abolished the directly political significance of social classes; i.e. 'social classes', not 'Estates', exist now. Hegel underestimated the enormous historical change which had taken place.

Hegel's attempt to conflate 'Estates' and 'classes' had some basis in contemporary linguistic usage. At the time "Staende" referred to both, as Hegel himself noted in a passage that perfectly reveals the problem. After mentioning individualistic, liberal political thought, he argued:

> So-called 'theories' of this kind involve the idea that the classes [Staende] of civil society and the Estates [Staende], which are the 'classes' given political significance, stand wide apart from each other. But the German language, by calling them both *Staende*, has still maintained the unity which in any case they actually possessed in former times.[13]

But, as Marx pointed out, Estates and classes are based on very different social arrangements. It is not that the German language contained the truth; it is rather that the German language had not yet caught up with social reality, a situation soon remedied by the term 'Klasse'.

Hegel wanted to utilize the existing social distinctions in private life, to elevate them to the political sphere, thereby being able to most efficaciously bring to bear the universalizing capacities of the bureaucracy on the particularism of civil society. He wanted to provide an arena between civil society and the executive branch in which the particularism of civil society and the universality of the state could be fought out. In this way Hegel hoped to avoid the development of the usual stark opposition of a bureaucracy immediately confronting civil society as a coercive force, with mutual incomprehension and antagonism.

The expected response to Hegel's proposal is that this will simply reintroduce class distinctions into the political sphere, corrupting the universality of the state by particular interests. The common interpretation of Marx's critique of Hegel is precisely that. However this interpretation is only partly correct. Certainly Marx was aware of the problem of 'corruption' of universality but he was not very concerned with it in his criticism of Hegel. Rather than merely restate liberal critiques Marx presented a very surprising thesis: the social distinctions upon which Hegel wished to construct his 'Estates' are not important enough to bear the weight. In this early work Marx argued that *modern classes are relatively unimportant*.

Marx believed that there are no social distinctions in modern society that are so well-demarcated and lasting that a new Estates system could arise. Modern social distinctions do not serve as the basis of limited communities as they did in the Middle Ages.

> The present state of society is distinguished from that which preceded it by the fact that civil society does not sustain the individual as a member of a community, as a communal being. On the contrary, whether an individual remains in a class or not depends partly on his work, partly on chance. The *class* itself is now no more than a *superficial* determination of the individual, for it is neither implicit in his work, nor does it present itself to him as an objective community, organized according to established laws and standing in a fixed relationship to him.[14]

In a manner reminiscent of Weber, Marx went on to remark that 'class' and 'social position' differ in modern society, reducing the salience of class.

Marx's criticism of the Estates here is purely negative. He as yet had no positive conception of social classes. When he used the term he had in mind the social groups of the Middle Ages which were the basis of Estates. In contrast the chief characteristic of modern civil society is the privatization of social life. Society stripped of its immediate political importance becomes "fluid" and ever-changing:

> civil society exists as the *class of private citizens*. Class distinction is here no longer a distinction between autonomous groups distinguished by their *needs* and their *work*. The only universal distinction to survive is the superficial and formal one of the difference between town and country. Within society itself, however, distinctions are variable and fluid and their principle is that of *arbitrariness*. The chief criteria are those of *money* and *education*. ... The principle underlying civil society is neither need, a natural moment, nor politics. It is a fluid division of masses whose various formations are arbitrary and without organization.[15]

Marx's extreme view here is seen in his characterization of even the distinction between town and country as "superficial".

According to Marx, when the Estates of the Middle Ages dissolved, civil society became the sphere of "individualism".

> The civil society of the present is the principle of *individualism* carried to its logical conclusion. Individual existence is the ultimate goal; activity, work, content, etc. are only means.[16]

With the dissolution of the autonomous communities of the Middle Ages the principle of civil society is no longer communal activities but "enjoyment and the capacity to enjoy."[17]

From the above it is seen that it is entirely false to view this early work of Marx as containing the germ of his theory of social classes. Marx is here one of the greatest critics of the conception of classes because he was intent on destroying any basis for the revival of the Estates system. Marx only had in mind the old social formations which were the basis of the Estates and that is the referent of the word 'class' (Stand). The proof of this lies in his appraisal of the working class as "not so much ... a class of civil society as ... the ground on which the circles of civil society move and have their being."[18] Marx was only beginning to puzzle over the proletariat.

Although Marx did not have a conception of social classes in his early work, the above discussion is important in a number of ways for his later analyses. First, the dissolution of the Estates leads to a radical separation of civil society and the state. A reunion of these two spheres is not possible through a revival of the Estates system. The modern state which emerges therefore stands in a drastically different relation to society than previous forms and the specificity of the modern state rests on this separation.

Secondly, a corollary of the above, modern civil society provides no stable social formations that can be *immediately* expressed in the political sphere. Since there are no autonomous, pre-political communities in modern society, the structure of the modern political apparatus cannot be based directly on distinctions in civil society.

This point is very important. Marx later rejected the idea that there are no social distinctions that are politically relevant. But he never rejected the idea that these formations *do not form communities* on the level of civil society. His later formulation is that the modern state *as a whole* is the mediated expression of the economically dominant class, or better, the economically dominant class can only act as a *class* through the mediation of the state. The difference between Estates and 'classes' (in his later sense of the term) is that the former exists as a community, a corporate entity. The latter, however, must be *made* a corporate entity through the mediation of political institutions.

Marx's general critique of Hegel's Estates is crucial to understanding the theory of classes developed later and how they are related to the specific structure of the modern state. However Marx also developed other criticisms of Hegel in the *Critique* which are especially important for illuminating Marx's conception of the transcendence of the state. It is worthwhile to examine these more specific arguments, not least of all because they lead eventually to the first formulation of the idea of the transcendence of the state.

Marx rejected Hegel's proposals for the two Estates, the landed Estate and the business Estate, in different ways. Briefly, the landed Estate cannot mediate even on Hegel's terms because its political expression is too concrete; the business Estate cannot mediate because its political expression is too abstract. Both of these discussions help delineate the specific character of the modern state and the possibilities and requirements for transcending it.

Marx's analysis of the basis of the landed Estate in primogeniture is well-known but often somewhat misconstrued. It is generally regarded as an early argument that private property corrupts the state, and the subsequent argument that class interests based on private property form the content of the state. This is an aspect of Marx's discussion, of course (an obvious one), but not the central point. Marx was concerned to lay bare the *structural* bases of the modern state, therefore his analysis of primogeniture is not so much an analysis of private interests but of the structural bases of political alienation.

The alienation caused by primogeniture is twofold. First, landed property bound by primogeniture cannot be exchanged, therefore it does not enter into social intercourse: it is alienated from society. It stands apart from the flux of social affairs, which was precisely Hegel's intention: to produce an element of the state which could not be buffeted by the waves of economic movement. (Marx pointed this out as a contradiction by Hegel who had earlier defined 'property' by its alienability.)[19] Because of its separation from the movement of civil society, Marx called property based on primogeniture "the superlative form of private property, private property supreme,"[20] -- 'supreme' in that it has no social connections.

Secondly, primogeniture alienates property from its nominal owner by depriving him of the 'right of use and abuse'. Private property is not bound to its owner; the owner is bound to his property.

> *The 'inalienability' of private property implies the 'alienability' of the universal freedom of the will and of ethical life.*[21]

Marx was not yet making an argument against private property in general, as is commonly supposed, but against a particular form of private property. This is revealed by his contrast of primogeniture with the property of the business classes:

> in all these relations the *human* heart can be heard throbbing behind the facade of property, in all of them we witness man's dependence on man. Whatever the nature of this dependence it is *human*, unlike the situation of those slaves who, because they are not bound to society but to the *soil*, imagine themselves free; freedom of the will in these circumstances amounts simply to the *absence* of any content but that of *private property.*[22]

Both are forms of *private* property, therefore both contain alienation and unfreedom, but Marx was intent on criticizing primogeniture, not private property in general.

Marx's analysis of primogeniture is not important as a conception of private interests corrupting the state, but because it connects private property and alienation. As will be shown later, one of the definitions of the transcendence of the state is the overcoming of alienation. Since private property is necessarily a structure of alienation, private property must be overcome. It is not because class interests based on private property corrupt the universality of the state that private property must be abolished. Rather it is because private property is a structure of alienation intimately related to the alienation of the state from society that private property must be destroyed in order for the state to be transcended.

The structure of private property produces the specific form of the capitalist state *before* distinct class interests emerge, when private property ceases to serve a progressive function. Private property as an alienating structure is primary; class interests based on private property are secondary. Marx's analysis of primogeniture is an advance precisely in that it brings out the objective structure of private property (albeit only in a germinal form) and because it avoids the liberal preoccupation of protecting the universality of the state from corruption by private interests. Unlike for Marx, this preoccupation is a permanent one for liberal thinkers because they intend to leave intact the social structure which gives effect to private interests.

Marx's specific criticism of Hegel's business Estate is different from the critique of the landed Estate, but it also leads into a discussion that is important for understanding the theory of the transcendence of the state: an analysis of 'representation'. Marx desired here to merely make additional arguments about the separation of civil society and the state but he raised issues that bear directly on his later discussions.

As previously mentioned, Hegel proposed that the business Estate be composed of representatives of the corporations, forming the lower house of the legislature. Marx's specific arguments against Hegel are not so important as the occasion this provided for a general rumination on the failings of the 'representative state'.

In an argument that was to be central to Marx's conception of the state, he explained that the separation of civil society and state creates the "representative state", i.e. the state as a sphere of universality separate from and counterposed to the particularity of civil society. The establishment of a well-developed representative state is preferable to the illusory formulations of Hegel (who only wanted representation of corporations and only applied this to the lower house) because it clearly shows the problems of the modern state in general.

> The representative constitution is a great advance because it is the *open*, *logical* and *undistorted* expression of the *situation of the modern state*. It is an *undisguised contradiction.*[23]

The 'contradiction' is that the modern state is separated from civil society, dividing each human being into a private and public self with no real connection between the two. Hegel, of course, recognized this and his philosophy is an attempt to provide the connection. Marx saw this clearly, remarking that "the deeper truth" is that Hegel "experiences the separation as a contradiction,"[24] but instead of seeking a real solution Hegel settled for the "semblance of a resolution."[25] The separation of civil society and the state rests on the privatization of social life; Hegel's "reminiscences" do not resist this tendency but neither does the representative state.[26]

Marx argued that humans are essentially communal beings[27] and the proper state is one in which this social quality is realized. Since Hegel insisted on keeping civil society and the state apart, assigning each its sphere of action, the real life of the individual cannot achieve political expression.

> He can advance to the status of *citizen of the state* only as an *individual*, i.e. in contradiction with the *only available forms of community*. His existence as a citizen of the state is one which lies beyond the scope of his existence in any *community*, i.e. it is entirely *individual.*[28]

Torn from his real social ties, that which determines what he is, the individual is an abstraction.

> The people thus appear trussed and dressed and devoid of any recognizable character, as they must be if they are to be integrated into an organic state.[29]

Hegel's complex mediations are no answer. Either the individual achieves political expression just as he is, as a member of civil society, or the state as a community will never be a reality. One can only create a state directly from existing communities, such as they are.

Marx's basic point on representation is simply that a number of questions that puzzle political theorists, e.g. the 'delegate/trustee' dilemma,[30] presuppose the separation of civil society and the state and will disappear with this separation. However, Marx's preliminary criticisms of representation are somewhat shallow. He believed that Hegel's 'deputies' of civil society who are not bound by formal instructions are a contradiction: they are supposed to represent civil society and the universal interests of the state at the same time. Marx is correct but he failed to see that this contradiction is not a logical lapse by Hegel: 'representation' itself is a contradictory concept.

In its most general meaning 'representation' is 'to be present and not present at the same time' or, more ambiguously, to be present 'in a sense'. 'Representation' is the concept through which we attempt to comprehend the separation of state and society, and different conceptions of representation depend upon how one views this separation. Marx was correct in linking the contradictory notion of 'representation' and the contradictory demands of the state/society division, but he did not struggle with the issue for long: he side-stepped it.

Marx argued that even the most perfect representative system, one which would allow everyone the opportunity to become a representative, is necessarily flawed. Instead of allowing all to substantially participate in the universality of the state, representation is the delegation of universality to a restricted group.

> The separation of the political state from civil society takes the form of a separation of the deputies from their electors. Society simply deputes [*sic*] elements of itself to become its political existence.[31]

Even a completely meritocratic system is no substitute for abolishing the separation of civil society and the state.

> The *opportunity* to join the class of civil servants, available to every citizen ... is highly superficial and dualistic in nature. Every Catholic has the opportunity of becoming a priest (i.e. of turning his back on the laity and the world). Does this mean that the priesthood ceases to be a power remote from Catholics? The fact that everyone has the opportunity of acquiring the right to *another* sphere merely proves that *his* own sphere does not embody that right in reality.[32]

Rather than deputizing certain elements of civil society to act for the universal interest (in either of Hegel's two ways, Estates or universal class), *all* must become members of the universal class and this necessitates the dissolution of the form which restricts universality to a particular group.[33]

Occasionally Marx seems to argue that the modern political form is to some extent *responsible* for the atomism and particularity of civil society. Most thinkers justify the independent state by referring to the fragmentation of civil society, but Marx hinted at this more interesting view. Although the divisions of civil society no doubt result in the creation of a separate political sphere embodying universality, this restriction of universality may further increase the particularity of civil society.

> The atomism into which civil society is plunged by its *political* actions is a necessary consequence of the fact that the community, the communistic entity in which the individual exists, civil society, is separated from the state, or in other words the *political state is an abstraction* from civil society.[34]

Representation of individuals torn from their real-life communities in civil society increases the atomism of civil society. A political apparatus based on the 'abstract individual' can only produce an abstract 'state'.

The abstraction of the state, its separation from real life, causes the people to be generally uninterested in its affairs.

> Of all the different expressions of the life of the people the political state, the constitution, was the hardest to evolve. When it did appear, it developed in the form of universal reason opposed to other spheres and transcending them. The task set by history was then the reclamation of universal reason, but the particular spheres do not have the feeling that their own private existence coincides with the constitution or the political state in its transcendent remoteness, or that its transcendent existence is anything but the affirmation of their own estrangement.[35]

The text is ambiguous but Marx seems to have been moving toward the position that when universality is restricted to a certain sphere, the particularity of civil society is reinforced. This is an argument that has been pursued in different terms by later Marxists (e.g. Nicos Poulantzas). Marx's idea is that civil society and the state are *dialectical* opposites, i.e. each term interacts with the other such that they *reproduce* each other. The particularity of civil society and the state as universality emerge simultaneously from the dissolution of feudal political forms. Marx only elaborated this argument in "On the Jewish Question" and later works.

Many 'Marxists' would be uncomfortable with this argument because they insist on the causal primacy of social structure, whereas this viewpoint assigns a real efficacy and significance to political *form* itself in recreating the social formation. An analysis of political form (indeed, *political* theory) then becomes absolutely essential. Marx himself only touched on this problem in his critique of Hegel. Instead of pursuing it he put forth the argument that the only real answer to the political problems of modern society is the overcoming of the separation of state and civil society. The *name* Marx gave to this project is "democracy".

As is well-known, Marx's response to the problems of Hegel's political theory was a call for "democracy". This is the origin of the customary interpretation of the early Marx as a radical-democrat, not a communist.[36]

However Marx's use of the term is unusual: by "democracy" he meant the direct expression of the civil community in political life. Marx's general concern in using the term "democracy" was *not* with such issues as better representation tationtation(which he did not think would work), free elections, civil liberties, etc., that is, procedural questions. "Democracy" for Marx is nothing less than a demand for the end of the alienation of state and society. It is a call for their identity.

Hal Draper has reviewed the status of the word 'democracy' in Germany at the time.

> No word was in a greater state of flux and chaos than *democracy*. ...
> Especially on the radical end of the political spectrum, the word has
> a marked tendency to overlay its political content with a social one.
> ... it was widely used not so much for particular forms or procedures
> of government as for the *social content* of a regime: the extent to
> which the regime had a base in the people, regardless of how its pro-
> cedures reflected that base.[37]

Only by understanding Marx's unusual (from our perspective) use of the word 'democracy' can we make sense of certain phrases such as "democracy of unfreedom" and cast doubt on the common interpretation that he was at this time just another 'bourgeois radical-democrat'.

Marx noted that the separation of state and civil society in modern societies sharply distinguishes them from previous political forms. In ancient societies the state does not appear as a form whose role is to universalize an alien content (civil society).

> Either the res publica was the real private concern of the citizens, their
> real content, while the private person as such was a slave -- this was
> the case among the Greeks, where the political state was the only true
> content of their lives and aspirations ...[38]

or there was an Oriental despotism where caprice ruled undisguised by the figleaf of the 'general interest'.[39] Marx's account is somewhat romantic (in Athens there were private persons who were not slaves: resident aliens, i.e. 'metics') but his point is clear.

In the feudal state material affairs and political structure coincided but the state was divided among several autonomous communities, the Estates and corporations, and was 'unfree', i.e. all were bound by feudal obliga-

38

tions. Because of this division of the nation into various closed communities, Marx called the Middle Ages "the *animal history* of mankind, its zoology."[40] Since civil life and political life were identical in feudalism but all were bound to one another Marx also referred to the Middle Ages, in a very telling phrase, as the "democracy of unfreedom".

> In the Middle Ages the life of the people was identical with the life of the state. Man was the real principle of the state, but man was *not free*. Hence there was a *democracy of unfreedom*, a perfected system of estrangement.[41]

The problem for modernity is to unify civil and political life *and* create real freedom for all.

According to Marx, modern social conditions have established the possibility of the emergence of a "true state", the actualization of man's essence, universality and community,[42] because of the decline in the importance of class distinctions. Civil society is a community but a community alienated by the political sphere which confines universality to a particular sphere, or even (in Hegel) a particular class. Universal suffrage will make the civil community the real community because

> the *vote* is the *immediate, direct, not merely representative but actually existing* relation of civil society to the political state.[43]

"Universalization of the vote" is therefore the key issue in reform movements.[44]

We must be very precise: Marx was saying that universal suffrage will *realize* democracy, not '*is*' democracy. Democracy is the unification of civil and political life, not a set of procedures. Universal suffrage is a means, not an end. A nation can have democratic forms (e.g. the United States) and still not be a democracy in Marx's sense of the term. Rather, a nation with democratic forms that are still separate from civil society Marx called a "republic".

> In a democracy the *abstract* state has ceased to be the dominant moment. The conflict between monarchy and republic still remains a conflict within the framework of the abstract state. The *political* republic is democracy within the abstract form of the state.[45]

How a 'republic' can come about is unclear in this text. We could infer that Marx only introduced the distinction in order to show the difference between his use of the word 'democracy' and that of others, and possibly that he considered the republican form to be inherently unstable, as he did in his later works. The whole matter is clarified somewhat when we comprehend Marx's understanding of another key term, "suffrage".

The above argument by Marx is reinforced by his extension of the word "suffrage" itself. For Marx "suffrage" is not merely voting and then a return to one's civil concerns. Marx argued that to be a member of the state is to take a genuine interest in deliberating on matters of common concern, to regard the universal interest as one's particular interest. In this sense a person cannot 'want' to be a member of the state (as universal); either one *is* a member or one is not. Either one takes an interest in "deliberating and deciding on matters of concern" or one does not.[46]

> So that when we are speaking of *real* members of the state we cannot assert that they *ought* to participate in the affairs of the state. For in that case we would be talking about those subjects who *want* and *ought* to be members of the state, but *are not* in reality.[47]

When Marx argued for extension of the suffrage he was not merely speaking of voting rights, although the extension of voting rights is an important means for creating the kind of state he envisioned.

> What is crucial is the extension and the greatest possible *universalization* of the *vote*, i.e. of both *active* and *passive* suffrage.[48]

"Passive suffrage" means this general concern and participation of people in the affairs of the state. Passive suffrage exists when the universal interest is made a particular interest of individuals and *that* only happens when the particular interest of individuals in civil life becomes the universal interest, i.e. when the universal no longer stands opposed to the particular as an external form to an alien content. Voting rights are instrumental for bringing this about. The 'state' as universality can only be achieved by destroying the "strictly political state" as form, as 'representative' separate from society.

The above is quite abstract and one of the most convoluted passages in Marx's *Critique*. However it is extremely important for Marx's conception of the transcendence of the state. The context is a discussion of how many

40

people should participate in the legislature. Marx's response is that the whole issue presupposes the separation of state and civil society. If there is no distinction between the two, then everyone participates in the state but does not actually have to be a member of the legislature.

Marx's reasoning on this particular point is very ambiguous and he appears to ascribe a unity to civil society (once its separation from the political is overcome) that is unjustified. This of course follows from his earlier argument that the distinctions within modern civil society are politically irrelevant. He also overestimated the impact of voting for making the universal interest a particular concern. (It was not the last time he overestimated voting rights.) But his conception of a proper state and his very radical notion of democracy are evident.

"Democracy" is achieved in Marx's sense of the word when the separation of civil society and the state is overcome. "Unrestricted active and passive suffrage"[49] is brought about through electoral reform. But for Marx the implications of this reform are extremely profound:

> electoral reform in the abstract political state is the equivalent of a demand for its *dissolution* and this in turn implies the dissolution of civil society.[50]

The 'state' as universality will come about only with the abolition of the 'strictly political state' as a separate structure, and the abolition of one term is the abolition of its opposite, civil society.

The deep meaning Marx attached to the word "democracy" makes comprehensible his earliest formulation of the idea of the transcendence of the state.

> In modern times the French have understood this to mean that the *political state disappears* in a true democracy. This is correct in the sense that the political state, the constitution, is no longer equivalent to the whole.[51]

We must be careful in reading this passage. As Hal Draper has persuasively argued, here Marx affirmed certain things but rejected other implications.

> The first sentence is plainly an acknowledgement of the ideas about 'an-archy' (no state) emanating from Proudhon and others. But the second sentence refuses to go that route. In 'true democracy' the state will *not* entirely disappear but will only dwindle to its proper sphere;

it will no longer claim to run the whole but only to take care of one particular social task among other particulars ... It has a limited, not an unlimited, place in society.[52]

Draper's term "dwindle" is ill-chosen because it does not express the radical break this new form makes with the old. His word is an echo of his agreement with the later term 'withering away' and all of the assumptions underlying it. But he is right in pointing out that Marx's passage is a *correction* of 'anarchist' thought. From the beginning Marx's conception is distinct from the anarchists. 'Democracy' is not anarchy; it is the end of the 'representative' state, an institution standing in a superior relation to society as the embodiment of unity, community, and universality.

This "disappearance of the state" does not mean that an organ of specific policy formation and execution will disappear. But this function will no longer be privileged; as for Saint-Simon, it will merely be one function in a differentiated but unstratified division of labor. Marx was perfectly clear on this point:

> the *legislature* entirely ceases to be important as a *representative* body. The legislature is representative only in the sense that *every* function is representative. For example a cobbler is my representative tivetivein so far as he satisfies a social need, just as every definite form of social activity, because it is a species-activity, represents only the species. That is to say, it represents a determination of my own being just as every man is representative of other men. In this sense he is a representative not by virtue of another thing which he represents but by virtue of what he *is* and *does*.[53]

In a democracy for all to want to be legislators would be as foolish as for all to want to be cobblers. The legislator merely performs a different function in the division of labor, distinct but not distinguished. Marx presented precisely the same conception thirty years later in his struggle against the ideas of Bakunin.

To borrow a phrase, there is a specter haunting the *Critique*, the specter of Aristotle. In a letter written to Ruge during the same period as the *Critique* Marx said:

> A German Aristotle who wished to construct his *Politics* on the basis
> of our society would begin by writing 'Man is a social but wholly un-
> political animal'.[54]

In the *Critique* Marx agreed with Aristotle that the life proper to a human being, the life in which his essence is realized, is political life, which for Marx meant participation in the universality of the state. When a system is constructed in which all are involved in public affairs, that is, when all become 'political', the state as a separate and restricted embodiment of universality will be transcended. The difficulty is, of course, how to create this political existence for *all* (unlike Aristotle's Greece). Marx believed that this is possible under modern conditions, that at least the basis has been developed. He was to spend the rest of his life uncovering the structural barriers and structural possibilities for this kind of existence presented by capitalism.

Marx was soon to argue that the key to this transformation is the proletariat. In the *Critique* Marx did not yet understand the place nor possibilities of the proletariat nor have a clear conception of 'social classes' as distinct from 'Estates', and in his description of the proletariat we again see the ghost of Aristotle. In the *Politics* Aristotle distinguished between the "conditions" of a polis and the "integral parts" of a polis. There are activities (and people who perform them) which are necessary *conditions* for the existence of the polis but do not form a real part of a functioning polis, i.e. those who perform these activities do not participate in political affairs. "Farmers, craftsmen, and the general body of day-laborers" are necessary conditions of political life but are not allowed to participate.[55]

The similarity of this to Marx's description of the working class is too striking to be a coincidence. This odd 'class', not really a class of civil society but "the ground on which the circles of civil society move and have their being,"[56] is soon seen as the basis for radical transformation. When Marx began to comprehend the proletariat his theory changed course but the insights of the *Critique* were not discarded; they were simply incorporated into a more concrete and complex understanding of capitalist society and the capitalist state.

Marx produced several arguments in his early critique of Hegel's political philosophy which formed the basis for further development of his theory of the transcendence of the state. First, Marx grounded the structure of the state as universal representative of society, as discrete body standing apart from and acting for the whole, in modern conditions of society, especially in the collapse of the Estates system. It was perfectly natural that his attention should turn to the specifics of this society which condition this precise form of state.

Secondly, Marx presented the vision of a society in which all of its members engage in public affairs, calling this society "democracy" with "passive suffrage". Throughout his work Marx was inalterably opposed to a special institution or class administering the universal interest. Instead Marx insisted that a 'non-representative state' is possible and desirable, a 'state' in which a governing apparatus exists but does not stand in a superior relation to the rest of society. Like Saint-Simon, Marx believed that the governing apparatus could become a simple organ of the whole, performing just another function in the division of labor.

Thirdly, Marx conceptualized property as primarily a structure of alienation. He did not view property simply in its effects on motivation (i.e. in a subjective sense) but considered its relevance to be in its restriction of human activity and possibility. This conception of property later allowed him to escape the usual critique of the capitalist state which focuses on the 'corruption' of political life. Marx's conception is more profound in that considering property as an objective social structure relates it to other structures of alienation such as the state and the division of labor. The importance of this structural conception will appear later.

Finally, Marx presented his entire argument in these terms: the state and civil society are dialectical opposites, each reinforcing the other in its opposition. It is this opposition and its abolition to which the transcendence of the state refers. Oppositions are not resolved by abolishing one side but by destroying the basis of the opposition. Marx oriented himself to the possibility of the transcendence of the state in this way, regarding the 'state' and 'society' as parts of a whole, an internally differentiated totality.

It must be acknowledged that at times Marx appears to deny this truly dialectical opposition by assigning causal priority to social conditions. ('Vulgar' Marxists have their passages too.) However I believe that the examination of all of Marx's writings on the subject will establish that the dialectical approach is his predominant one. Failing that, it will at least be clear that the persuasiveness of his argument that stateless society can be achieved rests on the recognition that political structure is historically specific and that *this* specificity is bound to the specificity of the social structure. From this point of view, any serious change in social structure *necessarily implies* an alteration of the political structure. Any further comments on this score here will confuse more than clarify.

There are of course several immediate problems with Marx's analysis in the *Critique*. The most important is the assumption that, with the breakdown of the Estates, distinctions within society have become relatively unimportant. Marx consequently believed that community could be quickly achieved under modern social conditions. He did not yet comprehend social classes in contrast to Estates and this inflated his expectations for an immediate development of non-representative government.

Since Marx assumed the establishment of community once Estates were abolished, he could not at this point see the particular structures that produce the representative state nor the way in which the state maintains these structures. He had only an abstract conception of the socio-political institutions which could bring about 'democracy'. However, it should be noted that *in his very ignorance of the relevance of social classes* for the representative state Marx had already integrated into his theory of the transcendence of the state the idea of 'classless society': the absence of important social distinctions is necessary for the possibility of stateless society. Marx erred in thinking that this was already substantially achieved with the dissolution of Estates.

Marx was soon to expand his inquiry into the modern basis of the independent state in "On the Jewish Question" and other articles. Therein he discovered that the dissolution of Estates was not enough to produce community, that, on the contrary, their very dissolution meant an increase in the fragmentation of society and that this reproduces the state as the separate and privileged embodiment of universality. However it was not until the *Economic and Philosophic Manuscripts of 1844* that Marx was to ground the state (in an abstract and cursory manner) in the existence of modern social classes.

1. There are a few exceptions to this neglect of Marx's *Critique*. See Lucio Colletti, "Introduction" to *Karl Marx: Early Writings* (New York: Vintage Books, 1975); Lucio Colletti, *From Rousseau to Lenin: Studies in Ideology and Society* (New York: Monthly Review Press, 1972); Galvano della Volpe, *Rousseau and Marx and Other Writings* (Atlantic Highlands: Humanities Press, 1979).

2. *Hegel's Philosophy of Right*, translated with notes by T. M. Knox (London: Oxford University Press, 1967): section 267 (p. 163), section 273 (p. 176), and section 276 (p. 179). See also Z. A. Pelczynski, "The Hegelian Conception of the State," in *Hegel's Political Philosophy: Problems and Perspectives*, edited by Z. A. Pelczynski (New York: Cambridge University Press, 1971), p. 13.

3. Arthur F. McGovern, "The Young Marx on the State," *Science and Society* Volume 34, Number 4, p. 441. The anarchists, on the other hand, *did* drop the broader meaning: see the editorial note of Sam Dolgoff, *Bakunin and Anarchy*, edited and introduced by Dolgoff (New York: Alfred A. Knopf, 1972), p. 75.

4. Shlomo Avineri, *Hegel's Theory of the Modern State* (New York: Cambridge University Press, 1972), p. 93; see in general pp. 93-98.

5. Knox, *Hegel's Philosophy of Right*, section 189 (p. 126).

6. I have not followed tradition in capitalizing 'state'. In German, of course, all nouns are capitalized and the reasons for carrying this practice into English in this context are unclear to me.

7. The highest state of exigency is war, which preserves the "ethical health of peoples": Knox, *Hegel's Philosophy of Right*, section 324 (p. 210) and section 278 (p. 181). See Marx, "Critique of Hegel's Philosophy of Right," in *Karl Marx: Early Writings*, edited by Colletti, p. 78.

8. See G. Heiman, "The Sources and Significance of Hegel's Corporate Doctrine," in Pelczynski, *Hegel's Political Philosophy*, pp. 111-135.

46

9. Knox, section 303 (p. 198).

10. Marx, "Critique," p. 137.

11. Ibid., p. 138.

12. Ibid., p. 90.

13. Knox, section 303 (p. 198).

14. Marx, p. 147.

15. Ibid., p. 146.

16. Ibid., p. 147.

17. Ibid., p. 147.

18. Ibid., pp. 146-147.

19. Ibid., pp. 169-170.

20. Ibid., p. 168.

21. Ibid., p. 169.

22. Ibid., p. 170.

23. Ibid., p. 141.

24. Ibid., p. 141.

25. Ibid., p. 141.

26. Ibid., p. 149.

27. Ibid., pp. 77-78.

28. Ibid., p. 143.

29. Ibid., p. 134.

30. Ibid., pp. 193-194.

31. Ibid., p. 193.

32. Ibid., p. 112.

33. Ibid., p. 112.

34. Ibid., p. 145.

35. Ibid., p. 89.

36. Although a serious and probing examination of Marx's *Critique*, August Cornu merely repeats the usual analysis of this work as that of a radical-democrat. See Cornu, *The Origins of Marxian Thought* (Springfield, IL.: Charles C. Thomas, Publisher, 1957).

37. Hal Draper, *Karl Marx's Theory of Revolution* Volume 1, Book 1: *State and Bureaucracy* (New York: Monthly Review Press, 1977), p. 85.

38. Marx, p. 91.

39. Ibid., p. 91.

40. Ibid., p. 148. See also ibid., p. 175 and Marx, letter to Ruge (May 1843), in *Karl Marx: Early Writings*, p. 201 and 204.

41. Marx, "Critique," p. 90.

42. Ibid., p. 112.

43. Ibid., p. 191.

48

44. Ibid., p. 191.

45. Ibid., p. 89.

46. Ibid., pp. 187-188.

47. Ibid., p. 188.

48. Ibid., p. 191.

49. Ibid., p. 191.

50. Ibid., p. 191.

51. Ibid., p. 88.

52. Draper, *Karl Marx's Theory of Revolution*, Volume 1, Book 1, p. 90. See also, ibid., p. 93.

53. Marx, "Critique," pp. 189-190.

54. Marx, letter to Ruge (May 1843), p. 201.

55. *The Politics of Aristotle*, edited and translated by Ernest Barker (London: Oxford University Press, 1958), Book VII, Chapter IX, p. 303. There is a similarity also in Aristotle's remark in the same chapter, p. 301: "in democracies all men share in all functions."

56. Marx, "Critique," p. 147.

Chapter 3

Uncovering the Structural Separation of State and Society

In the works which succeed his critique of Hegel Marx began exploring the specific structures of society that engender the state as a separate institution. Throughout, Marx considered the state and society in their opposition, each depending on the other for its specific constitution. The goal is always to transcend the opposition by a new form which would comprise both. It is necessary to think of state and society as obverse sides of a single coin, a separation within a totality. It is only by doing so that we will avoid the interpretation that reduces politics to an epiphenomenon of autonomous social processes.

Marx's first important work after the critique of Hegel was "On the Jewish Question". As the previous work was a criticism of Hegel's response to the French Revolution, so "On the Jewish Question" is Marx's own critique of the ideas and constitution that resulted from the French Revolution. In this and other works Marx tried to show how the existing state is both constructed on and reinforces the anti-communitarian structures of society. By arguing the basis of the independent state in "the market and the conditions which give rise to it" Marx furthered his comprehension of the conditions necessary for the realization of stateless society.

Marx began by reasserting the origin of the modern state as a 'universality' in opposition to the 'particularity' of civil society. Modern life is bifurcated, not just in thought but in reality.

> It is only in this way, above the particular elements, that the state constitutes itself as a universality. ... Where the political state has attained its full degree of development man leads a double life, a life in heaven and a life on earth, not only in his mind, in his consciousness, but in *reality*. He lives in the *political community*, where he regards himself as a *communal being*, and in *civil society*, where he is active as a *private individual*, regards other men as means and becomes the plaything of alien powers. ... The state stands in the same opposition to civil society and overcomes it in the same way religion overcomes the restrictions of the profane world, i.e. it has to acknowledge it again, reinstate it, and allow itself to be dominated by it.[1]

This division of man into "his *public* and *private* self"[2] is nonetheless an advance, an "emancipation", but an emancipation which reveals the limitations of the modern state. "Political emancipation ... is the last form of human emancipation within the prevailing scheme of things."[3]

The modern separation of state and society is not without challenge. Especially in the period of the revolutionary emergence of the separation, the newly constituted 'political state' attempts to go beyond its essential limitations. Speaking of the French Revolution, Marx said:

> At those times when it is particularly self-confident, political life attempts to suppress its pre-supposition, civil society and its elements, and to constitute itself as the real, harmonious species-life of man. But it only manages to do this in *violent* contradiction to the conditions of its own existence, by declaring the revolution *permanent*, and for that reason the political drama necessarily ends up with the restoration of religion, private property, and all the elements of civil society, just as war ends in peace.[4]

Why this is so, why "permanent revolution" fails, is not immediately clear. The reasoning at this point appears to be purely logical: the political state cannot overcome its opposite without abolishing itself, an argument Marx made explicit a few months later.

Another reason the French state has failed to suppress its opposite, as Marx argued later in *The Holy Family*, is that the new dominant class did not desire to go beyond the purely 'political state', in contrast to its representatives (e.g. Napoleon), who regarded the state as an end-in-itself.[5] Marx's general understanding of the French Revolution (which he had studied intensively)[6] was that it was not really concluded until the bourgeoisie had thwarted the plans of both Napoleon and the Bourbons and established the limited republic in 1830. Marx was merely beginning the argument in "On the Jewish Question", concentrating on clearly delineating the separation of state and society, i.e. defining the 'political state'.

According to Marx, the separation of state and society is firmly established in even the "most radical" French Constitution, the Constitution of 1793: *The Declaration of the Rights of Man and the Citizen*. Marx argued that there is a conflict between the 'rights of the citizen' and the 'rights of man', a conflict that corresponds to that between state and civil society.[7] The rights of the citizen provide for the participation of each individual in the community embodied as the political state, whereas the rights of man are the rights of individuals as members of civil society.

For Marx the 'rights of man' give free reign to all those impulses which make community impossible. He singled out four key concepts for criticism, above all the concept of "liberty".

> The liberty we are here dealing with is that of man as an isolated monad who is withdrawn into himself. ... the right of man to freedom is not based on an association of man with man but rather on the separation of man from man. It is the *right* of this separation, the *right* of the restricted *individual*, restricted to himself.[8]

Here Marx took a clear stand on an important issue, the difference between what Isaiah Berlin calls "negative liberty" and "positive liberty".[9] To Marx the simple establishment of negative liberty gives legal sanction to forces which disrupt the community. Each individual must regard every other individual as a potential enemy, encroaching on his freedom. "It leads each man to see in the other man not the *realization* but the *limitation* of his own freedom."[10] By securing 'negative liberty' the state establishes particularity in civil society rather than furthering possibilities which would produce community. The establishment of 'negative liberty' reproduces the need for the state as the restricted embodiment of community, i.e. as 'political state'.

The conception of liberty in the French Constitution has a real, practical content. As Marx said in regard to the second key 'right', "the practical application of the right of man to freedom is the right of man to *private property*."[11] Here, pursuing the insights gained in his study of Hegel, Marx clearly identified one of the foundations of the modern state and modern society: the separation of state-as-community from all interference in the individual's acquisition and utilization of property.

> The right of private property is therefore the right to enjoy and dispose of one's resources as one wills, without regard for other men and independently of society: the right of self-interest.[12]

In regard to the other two important rights, equality and security, Marx argued that 'equality' is merely equal access to liberty as defined above and 'security' is merely security of the fruits of that liberty, i.e. property.

With the notion of 'security' Marx went beyond his critique of Hegel. For Marx 'security' is a very important concept for revealing the limitations of the 'political state' and for demonstrating its concrete relation to society. Instead of simply arguing the separation of state and society Marx insisted that the conception of the state in the French Constitution reduces the state to *mere* security of the "isolated monads" of civil society. Political life tends to lose even the illusion of real community and "declares itself to be a mere means whose goal is the life of civil society."[13]

Too often the import of this discussion is missed. Commentators frequently see here a foreshadowing of a conception of the state as in some sense an 'instrument' of classes. However Marx was actually presenting a double criticism of the modern state: not only is the state separated from society, constituting itself as a restricted community above the bellum omnium contra omnes, but the state is further conceived as a means to securing individuals in their isolation. "Community" itself becomes a *means* in modern society and in this way the very concept is impoverished.

Marx was outlining a profound thesis: the 'instrumentalist' conception of the state common to liberal theory and much 'Marxian' theory is a specific product of a particular historical development. Implicit in his criticism is a more developed conception of the capitalist state, an attempt to account for the structural bases which produce precisely the 'instrumentalist' view. Rather than projecting when the state will no longer be necessary as an instrument, Marx tried to discover the bases which *establish* this 'instrumentalist' state and argue the possibilities for an entirely different way of organizing the polity.

Marx explicated the genesis of this 'restricted community'/'instrumentalist' state as he did in the critique of Hegel, by contrasting it with feudalism. In feudalism 'civil society' had a directly political character:

> the elements of civil life such as property, family, and the mode and manner of work were elevated in the form of seignory, estate, and guild to the elements of political life.[14]

However this did not entail elevating them to matters of universal concern. Feudal society was fragmented, different parts forming closed societies against the others. The individual was not separate from the community but each community was separate from the state as a whole, i.e. the 'state' was not conceived as a community. The unity of the state was regarded as "the *special* concern of a ruler and his servants, separated from the people."[15]

The political revolution which destroyed all the partial communities constituted the state as (potentially) the universal community and the universal concern of the people. But the abolition of the previous, juridically established communities is the freeing of individuals *from* community. In order to grasp Marx's meaning it is necessary to reproduce this lengthy passage:

> The political revolution thereby *abolished* the *political character of civil society*. It shattered civil society into its simple components -- on the one hand *individuals* and on the other the *material* and *spiritual* elements which constitute the vital content and civil situation of these individuals. It unleashed the political spirit which had, as it were, been dissolved, dissected, and dispersed in the various cul-de-sacs of feudal society; it gathered together this spirit from its state of dispersion, liberated it from the adulteration of civil life and constituted it as the sphere of community, the *universal* concern of the people ideally independent of those *particular* elements of civil life. A person's particular activity and situation in life sank to the level of a purely individual significance. They no longer constituted the relationship of the individual to the state as a whole. Public affairs as such became the universal affair of each individual and the political function his universal function.[16]

But the constitution of the state as pure universality was also the constitution of civil life as unadulterated particularity. The freeing of civil society from its political relations "was at the same time the shaking off of the bonds which had held in check the egoistic spirit of civil society."[17]

There are two points which should be emphasized here. First, Marx did not conceive motivations to be prior to an alteration of practice. Rather the structuring of practice is the origin of anti-communitarian desires. The same relation applies to conjecture about stateless society: the structural question must be prior to the motivational one. The project must be evaluated by the possibility of altering the state/society relation (or, more precisely, abolishing the 'relation') such that new motivations can emerge, not by idle musing on 'the new communist man'. Questions of psychology are important but secondary to the discussion of the possibilities of structural change. They must be considered secondary if we are to avoid much groundless speculation and unfruitful argument.

Secondly, it is important to note that the creation of the "political state" is *simultaneously* the creation of modern civil society.

54

> The *constitution* of the *political state* and the dissolution of civil
> society into independent *individuals* ... are achieved in *one and the
> same act.*[18]

Just as the 'state' is not a transhistorical concept, neither is what is called
the 'economic'. The relation between state and economy is historically
specific because their very separation is an historical act. The implication
of this argument is that interpretations of Marx which assign the 'economic'
a transhistorical causal priority are misleading in that the economic as a separate sphere only appears with capitalism. This will be explained at length
later. The crucial point here is that Marx conceived 'civil society' and the
'state' as emerging from a previous unity of some kind.

After these somewhat abstract explorations, in the second part of the article Marx discussed more concretely the bases for the separation of state
from civil society. The most important bases are the existence of the market
and money. The dissolution of earlier communities reduced the relation between individuals to a 'cash nexus'. Marx directly connected this to the
separation of state and society.

> *Practical need, egoism,* is the principle of *civil society* and appears
> as such in all its purity as soon as civil society has fully brought forth
> the political state. The god of *practical need and self-interest* is
> *money.*[19]

The concentration of universality in a separate structure is the freeing of the
members of civil society from any concern for the community in their daily
lives; their 'baser' instincts and desires are unleashed.

> Political emancipation was at the same time the emancipation of civil
> society from politics, from even the *appearance* of a universal con-
> tent.[20]

Marx proceeded to give the well-known argument that monetary relations
make all things an object of commerce. All relations among men become
external to the individual with the dissolution of previous communities and
this alienation becomes concretized in market relations: "Selling is the practice of alienation."[21] Marx added parenthetically that unrestrained self-interest destroys any objective basis for morality, that it becomes merely "formal".

Finally, Marx indicated that Christianity is the theoretical completion of this new order.

> Only under the rule of Christianity, which makes *all* national, natural, moral, and theoretical relationships *external* to man, could civil society separate itself completely from political life, tear apart all the species-bonds of man, substitute egoism and selfish need for those bonds and dissolve the human world into a world of atomistic individuals confronting each other in enmity.[22]

Whether Christianity is a *cause* of change is unclear but Marx seems to say that it does help to stabilize the new order. From his proposed solutions to the problem one can infer that Marx did not ascribe causal power to religion because he spoke of eliminating the *conditions* of religion, thereby making this kind of consciousness "impossible".

There is evidence that Engels was working in the same direction as Marx around this time, but of course independently of him. In an article published nine months after "On the Jewish Question" Engels also connected Christianity to 'atomism', money, and, interestingly, the transcendence of the state.

> The Christian state is merely the last possible manifestation of the state; its demise will necessarily mean the demise of the state as such. The disintegration of mankind into a mass of isolated, mutually repelling atoms in itself means the destruction of all corporate, national, and indeed of any particular interests and is the last necessary step towards the free and spontaneous association of men. The supremacy of money as the culmination of the process of alienation is an inevitable stage which has to be passed through, if man is to return to himself, as he is now on the verge of doing.[23]

As a matter of record, however, we must note that Engels' view of Christianity and its relation to the possible transcendence of the state was not always wholly negative. In *The Peasant War in Germany* he mentioned Thomas Munzer as prefiguring modern communist ideas:

> By the kingdom of God [on earth] Munzer meant a society with no class differences, no private property, and no state authority independent of, and foreign to, the members of society.[24]

Although several of the arguments and even phrases of these early works (e.g. "free and spontaneous association of men") play a role in the later formulations of the theory of the transcendence of the state, Marx and Engels soon dropped the religious criticism as a part of the theory as their political opponents changed from the Left-Hegelians to the anarchists.

In "On the Jewish Question" Marx argued that in order to overcome the division of state and society the "market and the conditions which give rise to it" must be abolished.[25] This would realize the goal he expressed in the first part of the article and was to repeat in similar terms twenty-seven years later in *The Civil War in France*:

> Only when the real, individual man resumes the abstract citizen into himself and as an individual man has become a *species-being* in his empirical life, his individual work, and his individual relationships, only when man has recognized and organized his *forces propres* [own forces] as *social forces* so that social force is no longer separated from him in the form of *political* force, only then will human emancipation be completed.[26]

This is the second clear statement that the state must be and can be transcended. Marx characterized the Paris Commune of 1871 in precisely these terms: the 'reabsorption of political force'. In the next year Marx gave the separation of state and society, and what is necessary for its transcendence, much firmer theoretical ground than simply the "market" by seriously exploring "the conditions which give rise to it."

After identifying market monetary relations as the source of disruption of community and firmly basing the existence and extension of these relations in the separation of state and society, Marx concentrated his attention and his studies on the anatomy of the market. In doing so he made two discoveries which are relevant to the theory of the transcendence of the state. First, and somewhat prematurely, Marx proposed the proletariat as the agent of revolution. In his critique of Hegel Marx had puzzled over the proletariat and five months later in the famous "Introduction" to the *Critique* he was still unsure how to characterize it. However he believed that the existence of the proletariat was definite proof of the "dissolution of the old order" and, as the 'most suffering class', *one* of the agents of its overthrow. (The other agent was "philosophy", i.e. philosophical communists like Marx.)

Marx was still unclear about the proletariat because he had not yet formulated a new conception of social classes; he was directly between the
'Estates' conception and a new conception. For this reason he called the
proletariat:

> a class of civil society which is not a class of civil society, a class
> which is the dissolution of all classes, a sphere which has a universal
> character ...[27]

In this passage Marx expressed two things: one, that the proletariat is the
definite dissolution of previous "classes" (i.e. 'Estates') and, two, that the
proletariat contains the "secret" of a new order. For the rest of his life Marx
contended that the abolition of the proletariat is *necessarily* the abolition of
all classes. Discovering this 'necessity' in the structure of the proletariat is
essential for understanding Marx's confidence in the future development of
stateless society.

The second consequence of Marx's concentration on political economy
was a fuller comprehension of the basis of the market. In his studies,
recorded in the *Excerpts from Mill* and the *Economic and Philosophic
Manuscripts of 1844*, Marx moved away from considering the market, the
sphere of circulation of capital, as the key to social and political structures
and examined the basis of the market in the sphere of production. The
division of labor, i.e. the specific structure of production, was now recognized as the origin of disruption of community.

In the *Excerpts from Mill* Marx continued arguing the deleterious effects
on community which result from exchange relations but he also insisted on
two new insights. First, he stated that production is the basis of exchange
relations and exchange society can only be abolished through the abolition
of the productive process as it is presently constituted, replacing it with
production consciously mediated by society.[28] Secondly, he argued that
community actually always exists, it just exists in alienated forms. Marx no
longer saw society as a pure bellum omnium contra omnes; rather, people
are always associated with one another through the interdependence of their
production.[29] Community need not be created; it needs to be consciously
appropriated and controlled by making production *consciously* social.

In the *Economic and Philosophic Manuscripts of 1844* Marx pursued
the basis of market relations in the sphere of production, especially analyzing capitalist production as "estranged labor". Marx argued that the specific

58

basis of capitalism in "estranged labor" is the source of all alienation and he firmly grounded liberation from alienated forms in the emancipation of the proletariat, providing a foundation for his earlier assertion of the role of the proletariat in the "Introduction" to his critique of Hegel.

The emancipation of the proletariat implies universal emancipation because:

> the whole of human servitude is involved in the relation of the worker to production, and all relations of servitude are nothing but modifications and consequences of this relation.[30]

This passage has been ignored in virtually all commentary on Marx's theory of the transcendence of the state. It is in the immediate relation of the worker to production that the possibility of stateless society must be sought. Unfortunately, again Marx did not elaborate here; this is simply more evidence of the "secret" of the proletariat.

There is one explicit statement in the *Manuscripts* of the transcendence of the state, remarkably similar to previous and later formulations of a kind of 'reabsorption' of the state.

> The positive supercession of private property, as the appropriation of *human* life, is therefore the positive supercession of all estrangement, and the return of man from religion, the family, the state, etc. to his *human*, i.e. *social* existence.[31]

Once more Marx merely indicated the relation between this and the overcoming of estranged labor; he did not offer an extended discussion.

There are two other early works which should be mentioned in this place: *The Holy Family* and "Critical Notes on 'The King of Prussia and Social Reform'." The former only contains a few pithy remarks on the relation of state and civil society but the whole of the "Critical Notes" is on politics. Therein Marx returned to the discussion of "On the Jewish Question" on the universality of the state as the dialectical opposite of the particularity of civil society and went a step beyond his previous analysis:

> the state is based on the contradiction between *public* and *private life*, between *universal* and *particular* interests. For this reason the state must confine itself to *formal*, *negative* activities, since the scope of its power comes to an end at the very point where civil life and work

begin. ... the *law of nature* governing the administration is *impotence.*
For the fragmentation, depravity, and *slavery of civil society* is the
natural foundation of the modern state, just as the civil society of
slavery was the natural foundation of the state of antiquity. The existence of the state is inseparable from the existence of slavery.[32]

Aside from the questionable historical analogy, Marx firmly integrated here
his conception from the *Manuscripts* that the modern state is structurally
related to the existence of "wage-slavery".

The issue under discussion was the effectiveness of the modern state to
handle social problems. In contrast to the liberal Bauer, Marx argued that
the modern state is impotent in regard to the problems of civil society because of its radical separation from civil society. In order to solve such
problems the state would have to go beyond itself as constituted and challenge its own conditions of existence.

If the modern state desired to abolish the *impotence* of its administration it would have to abolish contemporary *private life.* And to
abolish private life it would have to abolish itself, since it exists only
as the antithesis of private life.[33]

To end its impotence the state would have to call into question its fundamental basis, that is it would have to question "the *principle of the state,* ... the
actual organization of society of which the state is the active, self-conscious,
and official expression."[34]

According to Marx the political state *cannot* question its own basis; why
this is so is unclear. Marx tossed it off with the comment that "suicide is
contrary to nature", which is ironic because certain critics of Marx were to
say the same thing about the 'self-abolishing' transitional state of the passage to communism. In any case, Marx went on to say that the state explains
its impotence in solving social problems by referring to "administrative
defects" or "natural poverty".[35] However, it is actually constitutionally un-
able to get at the source of social problems because of the barrier of the
separation of state and society. The only alternative that remains for the state
is force and failure.

This discussion has a remarkably contemporary ring. When Marx argued about the state's explanation of its limitations and the *real* source of
these limitations in its structural separation from society, he could have been
as easily writing about existing socialist countries as about Prussia. The

source of many problems of socialist countries lies precisely in the failure to go beyond this, albeit modified, separation. That is, the origin of many problems of existing socialism lies in the fact that *the state has not been transcended.*

In the "Critical Notes" Marx reached two conclusions of relevance to our topic. First, social problems provide an objective basis for overcoming the present state because these problems will remain intractable until the state form is so altered. Political revolution is an essential aspect of social revolution.[36] Secondly, Marx stated in the strongest terms that if the separation of state and society is overcome and true community developed, that state will actually become "unthinkable".[37]

In these early works Marx firmly established the state as the dialectical opposite of society, deriving its separate existence from the specific structure of modern society and *reinforcing* this social structure by serving as its *complement.* His argument is somewhat difficult to follow because much of the explanation is purely logical, not empirical. It is also frustrating because he had two different aspects of the state in mind, the state as *idea* of universality and the state as a material embodiment of universality apart from society. For this reason it is common to regard Marx's early political arguments as mere criticism of an abstraction, i.e. ideological criticism. This is misleading and it does not allow us to see the relation between Marx's early conceptualization of the state and his later, more empirical analyses. Certain parts of his political theory, especially the theory of the transcendence of the state, are thereby rendered incomprehensible.

Marx never discarded the conception of the state as 'idea' of universality. It is present in his other discussions of the state, although not necessarily easily noticeable. Throughout their work Marx and Engels retained a sense of what Engels called the state in 1886: "the first ideological power over mankind."[38]

1. Karl Marx, "On the Jewish Question," in *Karl Marx: Early Writings*, introduced by Lucio Colletti (New York: Vintage Books, 1975), p. 220.

2. Ibid., p. 222.

3. Ibid., p. 221.

4. Ibid., p. 222.

5. Karl Marx and Frederick Engels, *The Holy Family, or Critique of Critical Criticism* (Moscow: Progress Publishers, 1975), pp. 145-146.

6. David McClellan, *The Thought of Karl Marx: An Introduction* (London: MacMillan Press, Ltd., 1972), p. 197.

7. Marx, "On the Jewish Question," pp. 228-230.

8. Ibid., p. 229.

9. Isaiah Berlin, *Four Essays on Liberty* (London: Oxford University Press, 1977), especially his "Introduction" and the essay "Two Concepts of Liberty".

10. Marx, "On the Jewish Question," p. 230.

11. Ibid., p. 229.

12. Ibid., p. 229.

13. Ibid., p. 231.

14. Ibid., p. 232.

15. Ibid., p. 232. This conception of the medieval state is quite similar to the view of H. C. Mansfield, Jr., "Medieval and Modern Representation," in *Representation* (Nomos X), edited by J. Roland Pennock and John W. Chapman (New York: Atherton Press, 1968).

16. Marx, "On the Jewish Question," pp. 232-233.

17. Ibid., p. 233.

18. Ibid., p. 233.

19. Ibid., p. 239.

20. Ibid., p. 233.

21. Ibid., p. 241.

22. Ibid., p. 240.

23. Frederick Engels, "Condition of England. 18th Century" [review of Carlyle's *Past and Present*], in *Marx-Engels Collected Works*, Volume 3 (New York: International Publishers, 1975), p. 476.

24. Engels, "The Peasant War in Germany," in *Marx-Engels Collected Works*, Volume 10 (New York: International Publishers, 1978), p. 422.

25. Marx, "On the Jewish Question," p. 241.

26. Ibid., p. 234.

27. Marx, "A Contribution to the Critique of Hegel's Philosophy of Right. Introduction," in *Karl Marx: Early Writings*, p. 256.

28. Marx, "Excerpts From James Mill's *Elements of Political Economy*," in *Karl Marx: Early Writings*, pp. 274-278.

29. Ibid., p. 265.

30. Marx, "Economic and Philosophic Manuscripts," in *Karl Marx: Early Writings*, p. 333.

31. Ibid., p. 349.

32. Marx, "Critical Notes on 'The King of Prussia and Social Reform'," in *Karl Marx: Early Writings*, p. 412. See also Marx and Engels, *The Holy Family*, p. 133.

33. Marx, "Critical Notes," p. 412.

34. Ibid., pp. 412-413.

35. Ibid., pp. 411-412.

36. Ibid., p. 420.

37. Ibid., p. 419.

38. Frederick Engels, *Ludwig Feuerbach and the Outcome of Classical German Philosophy* (New York: International Publishers, 1941), p. 54.

Chapter 4

The Division of Labor

In *The German Ideology* Marx and Engels developed their mature view of the structural bases of the state's existence and the broad changes that would be necessary for its transcendence. There are two interrelated structural bases: (1) the division of labor under capitalism produces the need for a separate institution embodying the 'general interest', and (2) this separate institution is necessary for classes to act on their class interests. Because the division of labor is the basis for the existence of classes, Marx and Engels concluded that the state will be abolished when the division of labor is abolished. The argument of *The German Ideology* is still somewhat abstract but this is because of its breadth. However, after exploring the argument in the broad terms of *The German Ideology* it will be necessary to explore more detailed discussions in other works which make the theory more concrete. This will be done in succeeding chapters.

The 'division of labor' is the primary concept of *The German Ideology*. Marx and Engels used it to explain 'classes', 'property', the 'state', and 'ideology'. Not surprisingly, the weight placed on the concept makes it difficult to sort out the specific relations it indicates. A brief outline of its range is therefore necessary.

There are three pairs of meanings of 'division of labor' in Marx's work, all of which are important in different ways for comprehending his theory of the transcendence of the state. The first pair of meanings is (1) a broad, historical use of the concept, applying to all ages and (2) a sense which is capitalist-specific, i.e. that only applies to the analysis of capitalism. The concept 'division of labor' is plagued by the same difficulties of other key concepts of Marx like 'class' and 'state': in some places it refers to a general historical phenomenon and in other places it has a capitalist-specific sense. Marx was not always true to the "principle of historical specification" that Karl Korsch rightfully claimed for him.[1]

The discussion of the transcendence of the state in *The German Ideology* for the most part utilizes only the capitalist-specific meaning of the 'division of labor'. It is only in its capitalist-specific sense that the division of labor could have the effects that Marx ascribed to it. Therefore for the moment we can neglect the broader historical usage of the term.

Within the capitalist-specific sense of the term there are also two distinct meanings: (1) the division of labor in society as whole and (2) the division of labor in the workshop. In the relevant passages of *The German Ideology* the 'division of labor' primarily refers to the structure of the capitalist productive and reproductive process *as a whole*. It therefore includes both production relations *and* relations of exchange. Marx later distinguished these two sets of relations by the terms 'relations of production' and 'sphere of circulation'. Correspondingly in *Capital* Volume One he distinguished two senses of the division of labor by referring to the "social division of labor" and the division of labor "within the workshop".[2]

However, in most of Marx's works the 'division of labor' is used in the expanded sense of the *social* division of labor. For example, in the *Grundrisse* Marx suggested that a 'division of labor' not mediated by exchange is not properly a 'division of labor' at all. Rather it should be called the "organization of labor".[3] Again, in *Capital* Volume One Marx stated that the division of labor mediated by exchange is just one form of cooperation and indicated that differentiation of tasks not based on exchange relations should not be referred to as the 'division of labor'.

The broad sense of the term 'division of labor' in *The German Ideology* and elsewhere is particularly useful for our purposes precisely because it comprises both the sphere of production and the sphere of circulation, i.e. exchange relations. The bases of the state and the specific meaning of 'classes' and 'property' can only be ascertained by considering the effects of *both* the relations of production and the exchange relations of capitalism. Both sets of relations create the need for a separate and independent institution charged with the function of unity of the social formation.

However, the division of labor "within the workshop" also plays a great role in Marx's theory of the transcendence of the state. Within this conception of the division of labor there is a third pair of meanings which John McMurtry has introduced in order to clarify Marx's argument in a key passage of *The German Ideology*. According to McMurtry we must distinguish between the 'division of task' and the 'division of the labor force', i.e. the distribution of individuals among the various tasks. His distinction is not only sound but extremely important for interpreting Marx correctly. I will introduce it in the proper place.

Of course ultimately it is impossible to eliminate all of the ambiguity of the concept 'division of labor' in Marx's work. It is futile to seek consistency where it is lacking. My only intention is to clarify the relation of the several senses of the division of labor to the existence of the state and classes and therefore their relation to the possible transcendence of the state.

The first part of the argument of *The German Ideology* which bears on the theory of the transcendence of the state concerns the social division of labor. Here Marx and Engels provided a concrete basis in production relations for the 'universality' of the state, in contrast to the more abstract, logical argument of Marx's early works.

> [T]he division of labor also implies the contradiction between the interest of the separate individual or the individual family and the common interest of all individuals who have intercourse with one another. And indeed, this common interest does not exist merely in the imagination, as the "general interest", but first of all in reality, as the mutual interdependence of the the individuals among whom the labor is divided. Out of this very contradiction between the particular and the common interests, the common interest assumes an independent form as the *state*, which is divorced from the real individual and collective interests ...[4]

Marx and Engels go on to say that the state appears as an "illusory community", always intertwined with other ties such as "family conglomeration", "language", and "other interests".[5]

In another passage Marx connected this new formulation with his earlier discussions. He wrote in the margin of the manuscript:

> Just because individuals seek *only* their particular interest, which for them does not coincide with their common interest, the latter is asserted as an interest "alien" to them, and "independent" of them, as in its turn a particular and distinctive "general interest" ... [T]he *practical* struggle of these particular interests, which *actually* run counter to the common and illusory common interests, necessitates *practical* intervention and restraint by the illusory "general" interest in the form of the state.[6]

Here Marx conceived the state as both an ideological phenomenon (an "illusory community") and a material institution possessing "practical" force.

At this point Marx and Engels' account is little different from that of a liberal political theorist, with the interplay of 'individual' and 'general' interests. But there is one point that supercedes liberalism. The distinction between "common" and "general" interests is directly related to the idea that common interests can be acted on without taking the form of the 'state'. For Marx and Engels, the term "common interest" does not imply "state" whereas the term "general interest" does.

According to Marx and Engels it is the isolation of individuals by the division of labor and the subsequent fragmentation of interests which produce the state as an independent institution. There are real common interests linking individuals, resulting from their interdependence, but the isolation of individuals makes it impossible for them to act on these interests. A separate institution is therefore necessary which pursues the "general interest". The "common interest" and the "general interest" are distinguished by their respective locations, the former on the level of 'society' and the latter on the political level.

Marx was to return to this conception a few times, virtually repeating what is said here. For example, relating this *general* phenomenon to the specific overdevelopment of the French state Marx wrote:

> Every *common* interest was immediately detached from society, opposed to it as a higher, *general* interest, torn away from the self-activity of the individual members of society and made a subject of governmental activity ...[7]

Although the regime of Napoleon III may have intensified this development, Marx and Engels considered it a general phenomenon not just of France of but of all capitalist states.

In another place, in an argument immediately concerned with the transcendence of the state, Marx used very similar terms. In his answer to Bakunin's *Statism and Anarchy* Marx directly counterposed an abstract "people's will" and a concrete "real will", just as he counterposed an abstract (and independent) "general interest" and a concrete "common interest".

> With collective ownership the so-called people's will vanishes, to make way for the real will of the cooperative.[8]

Marx's argument is that only under certain circumstances does the "common interest" become an independent "general interest". The task, of course, is to analyze the specific conditions under which this 'alienation' takes place and to judge the possibilities of altering those conditions.

Thus far the discussion of the relation of the division of labor to the separation of the state appears to be applicable to other historical periods. However there are two things which indicate otherwise. First, it is assumed that only market relations connect the individuals isolated by the division of labor. Differing market positions are the major cause of the fragmentation of their interests. The relation described here between the division of labor and the state only applies to fully developed market societies, i.e. capitalism.

The second element of the discussion which limits it to a particular society is the existence of 'classes' in distinction from 'Estates'. 'Classes' are intimately bound up with the specifically capitalist division of labor and the use of the term 'classes' in *The German Ideology* is very important for comprehending the structural establishment of an independent 'state' form. Marx and Engels often used the term 'classes' in a much broader way, applicable to other societies than capitalism.[9] However it is only the capitalist-specific sense that enables us to capture the manner in which the structure of classes is related to the structure of a separate state institution.

Positions in the division of labor are not as isomorphic as they first appear. Although the division of labor generates isolation of individuals and the fragmentation of interests, the capitalist division of labor also creates certain common positions in the productive process as a whole. There is a cleavage between those who own property and those who do not. Members of 'classes' are identified by the objective position they have in relation to the means of production.

In *The German Ideology* Marx and Engels regarded classes as primarily objective, alien structures into which individuals are 'inserted'. "Classes" in this sense of objective structures are *not* considered 'agents' of the historical process. They are *not* the subjects of history: they are the objective basis for the creation of subjects (i.e. actors). An individual is a member of a class because of her or his objective position in the productive process, whether she or he is aware of this position or not. "Classes" are structures of alienation.

The isolation of individuals by the division of labor and the commonalities of certain positions in the division of labor, i.e. 'classes', are not mutually exclusive descriptions. Individuals are isolated and members of classes at the same time. The fact that individuals are isolated and simultaneously class-bound is precisely what distinguishes 'classes' from

'Estates'. Although 'Estates' were also based on the relation to the means of production, 'classes' do not form communities as did the 'Estates'. Since classes do not form communities whose position is immediately expressed on the political level, they need the *state* in order to be *constituted* as a community, i.e. in order to act on their class interests. The modern state is an objective structure which mediates between the individual and his or her class.

This basis for the separate institution called the 'state' is never argued in a detailed and coherent form, although there are references to it throughout the work of Marx and Engels. *The German Ideology* contains more passages presenting this thesis than any other work. Marx began the argument with a precise distinction between 'Estates' and 'classes'.

> By the mere fact that it is a *class* and no longer an *estate*, the bourgeoisie is forced to organize itself no longer locally, but nationally, and give a general form to its average interests.[10]

Because of the division of labor mediated by exchange, 'class' individuals are intensely competitive with each other. Their common class 'will' must be constituted juridically and enforced by a power that stands separate from them and above them.[11]

> [I]t is precisely because the bourgeoisie rules as a class that in the law it must give itself a general expression.[12]

In order to rule *as a class* individuals of a class must "constitute themselves as 'we', as a juridical person, as the state."[13]

The precise meaning of 'class' is only uncovered if one sees it in this relation to the division of labor. The concept 'class' and the concept 'division of labor' are inseparable. The division of labor under capitalism isolates individuals from each other and, by making the social character of their production depend upon individual acts of exchange, subjects them to 'alien' (uncontrolled) market forces. But further, when one looks closer at these exchange relations one sees that there are patterns of domination determined by whether one owns means of production or not. This individualized division of labor is also a *class* division of labor.

Marx only outlined the relation between 'classes' and 'division of labor' in *The German Ideology* but, nevertheless, it remained the most substantial treatment of the issue (excepting parts of the *Grundrisse*) in his work. He

was clear on the essential point: 'classes' are objective structures of alienation; they are not pre-constituted political actors who can wield the state as
an instrument. Rather they need the state in order to constitute themselves
as class actors and maintain the conditions of their exploitation.

The capitalist division of labor and the existence of classes are intimately linked with each other. As I argue later, the fragmenting, individualized
division of labor in which social production is mediated by the market is
the specific condition of the existence of bourgeois exploitation. In order to
abolish this exploitation it is necessary to abolish its condition of existence,
i.e. the division of labor. Classes and the division of labor are abolished
simultaneously.

The division of labor which necessitates a separate institution for the
'general interest' also produces classes. Therefore from the beginning the
'general interest' and 'class interest' are intertwined. Although Marx distinguished 'general interest' and 'class interest' they are no more historically distinct than 'division of labor' and 'classes'. The abolition of the division
of labor, the condition of existence of 'classes' in the precise sense (as opposed to 'Estates'), is also the abolition of the institutional form embodying the 'general interest'. For Marx, to say 'classless' is also to say 'without
a division of labor', and therefore to say 'stateless'.

These connections cannot be made perfectly clear without going beyond
the broad arguments of *The German Ideology*, which I do in the next two
chapters. In the present work Marx's attention was on the basic objective
structures which produce the state. Since he regarded 'classes' and the
division of labor as primarily objective structures of alienation, he passed
easily from one to the other in his prescriptions for what must be abolished
if communism is to be established.

More often than not Marx suggested that the abolition of the division of
labor is the key to communism because he believed it to include the abolition of classes. In all of the central passages in *The German Ideology* on the
transcendence of the state and the creation of communism Marx concentrated on the abolition of the division of labor.

> [P]revious revolutions within the framework of the division of labor
> were bound to lead to new political institutions; it likewise follows
> that the communist revolution, which removes the division of labor,
> ultimately abolishes political institutions ...[14]

In later works, however, Marx's emphasis is on the abolition of classes. That the abolition of the division of labor comprises the abolition of classes is clear. Why, on the other hand, the abolition of classes necessarily implies the abolition of the division of labor is unclear and is unapproachable as long as we conceive the abolition of classes in terms of legal 'ownership', rather than in terms of destruction of alienating forms of the productive process. This is essential to understanding why Marx considered the two expressions interchangeable.

The relation between the abolition of classes and the abolition of the division of labor is revealed in Marx's conception of "property". Each position in the division of labor is defined by a specific relation to the "material, instrument, and product of labor."[15] A person's position in the division of labor determines her or his power of appropriation of the product of the collective labor of society. For this reason Marx asserted an identity between the division of labor and property.

> Division of labor and private property are, after all, identical expressions: in the one the same thing is affirmed with reference to activity as is affirmed in the other with reference to the product of the activity.[16]

This argument is more recognizable if we see that what Marx referred to here as 'division of labor' he referred to later as "relations of production".

Following the classical economists, Marx defined "property" as "the power of disposing of the labor-power of others."[17] This 'disposal' takes an immediate and a mediated form. The capitalist, because of his particular position in the capitalist division of labor, *immediately* 'disposes' of the labor-power of others by commanding the labor process and appropriating the product of the laborer. This allows her or him to dispose of the labor-power of others in a *mediated* fashion by purchasing in exchange the products of labor of other branches of the division of labor.

The position in the division of labor of the capitalist allows her or him to dispose of a certain portion of the collective labor of society. One's class position is determined by one's ability to appropriate, which in turn is determined by one's position in the division of labor, i.e. the social productive process as a whole. In order to abolish classes, the division of labor must be restructured such that the power of private appropriation of collective labor is destroyed. In this, rather sketchy, way the abolition of classes entails the abolition of the existing division of labor. Because Marx assumed these connections, his emphasis in *The German Ideology* was not in terms of the abolition of classes but the abolition of the division of labor, for which 'classes' and 'property' are identical expressions.

According to Marx, any revolution that does not abolish the division of labor will merely lead to a new form of political domination. Until this abolition the function of unity will remain and have to be performed by the state. The "common interest" will assume a form independent of and superior to society, as the "general interest", and those whose positions in the division of labor give them control of production will continue to appropriate in their private interests, using the 'ideal community' to secure such appropriation.

The abolition of the division of labor is therefore the key to the transcendence of the state. By 'abolition of the division of labor' Marx meant two things, depending on different meanings of 'division of labor'. In the broad sense of the division of labor, comprising both the relations of production *and* mediation by exchange (i.e. the 'social division of labor'), 'abolition' refers in the first instance to the aboltion of exchange relations. As previously mentioned, in the *Grundrisse* Marx spoke of the end of the division of labor as abolition of exchange:

> Instead of a division of labor such as is necessarily created with the exchange of exchange values, there would take place an organization of labor whose consequence would be the participation of the individual in communal consumption.[18]

In this broad sense of the division of labor the abolition of exchange is the primary goal.

However in a more restricted sense of the division of labor that Marx also used, that of the division of labor 'in the workshop', there is an additional meaning of 'abolition'. This second sense of division of labor refers to the actual structure of the productive process and the differentiation of labor functions. The abolition of the division of labor in terms of restructuring the labor process is regarded as one of the most utopian aspects of Marx's theory and the most easily and frequently attacked. However most criticisms do not really comprehend Marx on this point, therefore we must be very precise in reproducing his argument.

The central passage in *The German Ideology* which brings out this aspect of the abolition of the division of labor is quite famous but still must be quoted in full here:

> the division of labor offers us the first example of the fact that, as long as man remains in naturally evolved society, that is, as long as a cleavage exists between the particular and the common interest, as long therefore, as activity is not voluntarily, but naturally, divided, man's own deed becomes an alien power opposed to him, which enslaves him, rather than being controlled by him. For as soon as the division of labor comes into being, each man has a particular, exclusive sphere of activity, which is forced upon him and from which he cannot escape. He is a hunter, a fisherman, a shepherd, or a critical critic, and must remain so if he does not want to lose his means of livelihood; whereas in communist society, where nobody has one exclusive sphere of activity but each can become accomplished in any branch he wishes, society regulates the general production and thus makes it possible for me to do one thing today and another tomorrow, to hunt in the morning, fish in the afternoon, rear cattle in the evening, criticize after dinner, just as I have a mind, without ever becoming hunter, fisherman, shepherd, or critic.[19]

The precise meaning of this passage has been explicated by a distinction made by John McMurtry. He points out that the common usage of the phrase 'division of labor' conflates two things: "division of task" and "division of *labor*" in a strict sense of "laborforce".[20] "Division of task" refers to the complex differentiation of functions that is part of any advanced economy. As the means of production increase, the productive process is broken down into its constituent elements. Where there was one function performed by an agent, there are now several functions performed by several agents. "Division of task" refers to the creation of new and distinct 'places' in the productive process as a whole.

"Division of *labor*", on the other hand, means the distribution of individuals among these different 'places' in the productive process, i.e. it means division of the laborforce. We must always distinguish the differentiation of functions in an advanced economy from the individuals who perform those functions. It may well be that division of *task* is essential to an advanced production system at the present time but it is possible that a confining division of *labor* is not.

When Marx wrote of the abolition of labor (in the sense we are now discussing it) he did not mean the abolition of the division of task. This is revealed in his most favored manner of expressing it as the abolition of "enslavement" to the division of labor. In the above passage the distinct roles of 'hunter', 'fisherman', 'shepherd', and 'critical critic' remain. What is abolished is the *confinement* of an individual to any particular role. Marx considered the differentiation of functions in production and the confinement of individuals to a particular function to be separable issues.

Marx's position is not all that different from Emile Durkheim who also proposed the abolition of the forced division of labor but not the abolition of function. In *The Division of Labor in Society* Durkheim called the forced division of labor "an abnormal form".[21] However Marx differed from Durkheim in that Marx suggested a permanent alteration of places rather than simply a first free choice of one's position in the division of labor. In *Anti-Duehring* Engels summed up his and Marx's position by embracing the utopian socialist proposal for "variation of occupation".[22]

Although Marx was not explicit, it is not difficult to see what he expected to follow from this abolition of the forced division of labor. It was supposed that alteration of positions will extinguish the residual fragmentation of interests based on having exclusive positions in the productive process. Further, the abolition of the division of labor is of course necessary for the development of individuality and the cultural development which is the requisite for the expansion of the productive forces. Finally, the abolition of the forced division of labor is essential for the ability of society's members to "absorb" the functions of the state.

The concept 'division of labor' was relatively new in Marx's day (McMurtry ascribes it to Adam Smith)[23] and therefore some confusion is to be expected. However I believe Marx's argument to be quite clear, at least on this latter point: differentiation of functions may be necessary but limitation of individuals to "one exclusive sphere of activity" is the mark of a society that does not control its own productive process.

The German Ideology presents the mature opinion of Marx on the structural bases of the state's existence. Whenever he discussed the transcendence of the state after *The German Ideology* these are the bases of the state which he singled out for destruction. However there are several problems with his analysis. It is obvious from the above that the relations between 'division of labor' (in its many senses), 'classes', and 'property' are only outlined here and Marx never really cleared up the confusion in his later works, including the *Grundrisse*. Many of the key passages are simply too compressed to allow us insight into the relationships.

Another problem of a different order is the unexplained relation of the *proletariat* to political institutions. Since the proletariat is also a 'class', in the precise sense of isolated individuals sharing a certain position in the productive process, they too should require a state in order to achieve collective action, at least in the first instance. In places Marx and Engels argued exactly this:

> every class which is aiming at domination, even when its domination, as is the case with the proletariat, leads to the abolition of the old form of society in its entirety and of domination in general, must first conquer political power in order to represent its interest in turn as the general interest, which in the first moment it is forced to do.[24]

This is, of course, the basis of Marx's argument for the transitional state and for the very ambiguous "dictatorship of the proletariat".

However, throughout the greater part of the work after *The German Ideology* Marx portrayed the proletariat as an essentially homogeneous class forged into a class actor *without* necessary political mediation. Marx usually presented the proletariat as merely giving itself "expression", in contrast to the bourgeoisie which needs the state to constitute itself as a collective subject. Whether the proletariat needs the state to constitute itself as a class subject or if it is already a subject which merely 'expresses' itself in politics is a fundamental problem for Marxian political theory which will be addressed below.

For all its ambiguity there are several theses in *The German Ideology* which are important for the theory of the transcendence of the state. First, Marx correctly indicated the relation between 'classes', 'property', and the 'division of labor' and the fragmentation which is an essential aspect of the existence of 'classes' in a capitalist-specific sense.

Secondly, Marx firmly portrayed classes as objective structures, not as historical subjects. Because they are objective structures of alienation, classes do not simply give themselves 'expression'. On the contrary, classes are only constituted as historical subjects through the mediation of the state. One of the primary functions of the state is to *organize* classes into historical actors. The meaning of the 'abolition of classes' lies specifically in the abolition of those conditions which engender these alien structures, i.e. the division of labor and property.

Finally, because Marx conceived the transcendence of the state as the abolition of alienating social structures the vision of communist society which emerges in *The German Ideology* is somewhat at variance with common conceptions. For Marx, communism is the collective control of human relations and their effects.

> The reality which communism creates is precisely the true basis for rendering it impossible that anything should exist independently of individuals, insofar as reality is nevertheless only a product of the preceding intercourse of individuals.[25]

Marx did not conceive communism as a harmonious economic system freed of its class distortions. Marx, here and in every other place, conceived communism as a collectively controlled society. Its relatively unproblematic character and productivity come from the power over social relations which have lost their alien, uncontrollable nature because the bases of alienation, variously called 'division of labor', 'property', and 'classes', have been abolished.

In *The German Ideology* the structural separation of the state from society is argued as resulting from the division of labor and the needs of classes (properly so-called) for political representation. This analysis is useful but is still too broad to fully reveal Marx's understanding of the necessity in capitalist society for an independent institution embodying community. Therefore the next two chapters examine Marx's elaboration in other works of the general argument presented in a compressed form in *The German Ideology*. Specifically, we must explore in more detail Marx's arguments of the necessity of the separation of state and society as it is grounded in (1) the particular structure of capitalist production and (2) the consequences of production mediated by exchange, i.e. the sphere of circulation.

1. Karl Korsch, "Leading Principles of Marxism: A Restatement," in *Three Essays on Marxism*, introduced by Paul Breines (New York: Monthly Review Press, 1972), pp. 16-25.

2. Marx, *Capital* Volume 1 (New York: International Publishers, 1974), pp. 350-359.

3. Marx, *Grundrisse*, translated and introduced by Martin Nicolaus (New York: Vintage Books, 1973), p. 172.

4. Marx and Engels, "The German Ideology," in *Marx-Engels Collected Works* Volume 5 (New York: International Publishers, 1976), p. 46.

5. Ibid., p. 46.

6. Ibid., p. 47. Certain additions of Marx or Engels can be distinguished by their respective handwriting.

7. Marx, "The Eighteenth Brumaire of Louis Bonaparte," in *Surveys From Exile: Political Writings Volume II*, edited and introduced by David Fernbach (New York: Random House, 1974), p. 237.

8. Marx, "Conspectus of Bakunin's *Statism and Anarchy*," in *The First International and After: Political Writings Volume III*, edited and introduced by David Fernbach (New York: Random House, 1974), p. 336.

9. The best example of Marx and Engels using the term 'class' in a transhistorical sense is in "The Manifesto of the Communist Party": "The history of all hitherto existing society is the history of class struggles." In *The Revolutions of 1848: Political Writings Volume I*, edited and introduced by David Fernbach (New York: Random House, 1974), p. 67. Another example is in "The German Ideology" where it is stated that women and children were originally "slaves', i.e. "property" of the man: in *Marx-Engels Collected Works Volume 5*, p. 46. Finally, throughout *The Origin of the Family, Private Property, and the State* Engels used 'class' to describe slave society and its emergence from primitive communism. The examples could easily be multiplied.

10. Marx and Engels, "The German Ideology," p. 90.

11. Ibid., p. 329.

12. Ibid., p. 92.

13. Ibid., p. 357.

14. Ibid., p. 380.

15. Ibid., p. 32.

16. Ibid., p. 46.

17. Ibid., p. 46.

18. Marx, *Grundrisse*, p. 172.

19. Marx and Engels, "The German Ideology," p. 47.

20. John McMurtry, *The Structure of Marx's World-View* (Princeton: Princeton University Press, 1978), p. 80 footnote. Also, ibid., p. 69 and pp. 224-225.

21. Emile Durkheim, *The Division of Labor in Society* (New York: The Free Press, 1964), pp. 374-388.

22. Engels, *Herr Eugen Duehring's Revolution in Science [Anti-Duehring]* (New York: International Publishers, 1976), p. 319.

23. McMurtry, op. cit., p. 80 footnote.

24. Marx and Engels, "The German Ideology", p. 47.

25. Ibid., p. 81.

Chapter 5

The Autonomy of State and Production Under Capitalism

In later works Marx detailed the structural bases of the state that he had only outlined in terms of the division of labor in *The German Ideology*. In the third volume of *Capital* Marx argued that the specific organization of production is the key to understanding political forms, including the capitalist form.

> The specific economic form, in which unpaid surplus labor is pumped out of direct producers, determines the relationship of rulers to ruled, as it grows directly out of production itself and in turn reacts on it as a determining element. ... It is always the direct relationship of the owners of the conditions of production to the direct producers ... which reveals the innermost secret, the hidden basis of the entire social structure, and with it the political form of the relation of sovereignty and dependence, in short, the corresponding specific form of the state.[1]

The particular nature of the capitalist state lies in its separation from the productive process, i.e. in the 'relative autonomy' of both the state and production. It is this exclusion of the state from direct control of production which establishes the precise character of the capitalist division of labor and the nature of 'classes' in the strict, historically limited usage of the term. All these things depend on the manner in which surplus labor is extracted in the capitalist mode of production.

According to Marx, any productive process contains three elements: the laborer (the direct producer), the means of production, and surplus labor. Under feudalism, the laborer, the serf, was in "possession" of the means of production.[2] He directed and controlled the productive process and appropriated the product. However, he did not "own" the means of production, the land; the feudal noble did. Therefore the serf had to surrender a portion of the surplus product to the legal owner of the land in the form of rent (in kind or, later, in money) or personal service on the lord's land. In either case it was surplus labor that was surrendered to the lord.

Since the direct producer remained in possession of the means of production, extraction of surplus labor was open and clear: it was external to the

82

process of production and appeared so.[3] This is the basis of the relations of servitude specific to feudalism.

> It is furthermore evident that all forms in which the direct laborer remains the "possessor" of the means of production and labor conditions necessary for the production of his own means of subsistence, the property relationship must simultaneously appear as a direct relation of lordship and servitude, so that the direct producer is not free; a lack of freedom which may be reduced from serfdom with enforced labor to a mere tributary relationship.[4]

Because the possessors of the land carried on production independently of the lord,

> surplus-labor for the nominal owner of the land can only be extorted from them by other than economic pressure, whatever the form assumed may be.[5]

The consequence of this is the intertwining or simultaneity of what a later age could distinguish as 'political relations' (lordship and servitude) and 'economic relations' (production and ownership). Or as the earlier Marx would say, there was an identity of state and society in that one's 'political' position was the same as one's social position. The sundering of these two relations (or the *creation* of *two* relations where formerly *one* existed) is the principal characteristic of the capitalist state.

Historically the basis of capitalism was erected with the dispossession of the mass of workers from independent means of production. This process has often been described but rarely as well as in the chapter on "Primitive Accumulation" in *Capital* Volume One. Under the impact of the discoveries of the fifteenth century, the international market expanded, creating new possibilities for production. Especially under the prodding of the merchants of the cities, all barriers to increased production were destroyed. In the countryside the rise of the price of wool and the enclosure of the common land led to the "transformation of arable land into sheepwalks,"[6] 'freeing' the inhabitants to seek employment elsewhere. The Reformation further increased property-less laborers by the confiscation of church lands and the dissolution of monasteries, coinciding with the dissolution of feudal retinues.

A few prosperous serfs became agricultural capitalists but most had to seek work in the cities. Restrictive guild organizations which limited production and the market by regulating employment were disbanded and expanded production gave work to the mass of laborers streaming in from the countryside. Finally, with the complete establishment of capitalism three major factors of production became commodities: land, labor-power, and money. The market developed extensively (more parts of the globe) and intensively (commodification of more things).

It is important to remember that Marx did not consider this transformation to be 'determined'. There were objective possibilities (expansion of the market, the germ of capitalist production in the cities) and a class that pushed for their realization, i.e. the bourgeoisie and 'new' nobility. But the vehicles for this transformation were legislation and force. Marx was very clear on this point:

> In actual history it is notorious that conquest, enslavement, robbery, murder, briefly force, play the great part.[7]

The establishment of capitalism depended on the creation of a market in labor-power, which in turn depended on the expropriation of workers of means of production. This expropriation "is written in the annals of mankind in letters of blood and fire."[8]

The conditions of capitalist production are created by force and political violence. However, once established, capitalism functions on its own basis with its own laws of reproduction. We must distinguish between the *origin* of capitalist exploitation and the actual functioning and reproduction of exploitation in the capitalist epoch.

> The capitalist system presupposes the complete separation of the laborer from all property in the means by which they can realize their labor. As soon as capitalist production is once on its own legs, it not only maintains this separation, but reproduces it on a continually extending scale.[9]

Paradoxically, capitalism, born of forced expropriation, excludes violence and the state from the productive process.

If the mode of extraction of surplus labor determines the general relationship between rulers and ruled, then the secret of capitalism is that the extraction of surplus labor is hidden in the production relation of capital and labor. By the free exchange of equivalents, the 'free' laborer ('free' of guild restrictions, feudal obligations, and property) places himself or herself in a relation through which surplus labor, in its capitalist phenomenal form of 'surplus-value', can be appropriated by those who own the means of production and therefore the product.

Marx's argument from here is justly well-known. The generation of surplus-value is a consequence of the difference between the 'exchange-value' of labor-power, determined by the value of the necessities required to recreate it, and the 'use-value' of labor-power in the productive process. Given that the cost of necessities is not too high, the value created by labor-power, under certain conditions, exceeds the exchange-value of labor-power. The use-value of labor-power is only manifested by its application to means of production which under capitalism are owned by another. The use-value of labor-power is not recognized by the laborer and is really of no concern to her or him. She or he is only concerned with the exchange-value of labor-power. After labor-power has been alienated in exchange, the use-value of labor-power reveals itself in the production of values over and above the values exchanged for it in the market.

This process of production of surplus-value is hidden from both the laborer and the capitalist by the manner in which the exchange is perceived. The participants view it as an exchange of 'things': the value of necessities for 'labor'. The capitalist especially sees it as the coming together of different factors of production, a joining that he or she initiates and organizes, each factor paid at its value. The surplus-value that emerges over the value of labor, raw material, and means of production consumed, is the value of the *owner's* contribution, "overlooking and management".[10]

However, as Marx explained, 'labor' is not a 'thing', and as a factor of production, cannot be assigned a value. It is an *activity*, "labor-*power*", and as such is the *source* of all value. With the exclusion of the majority from means of production, its exercise creates use-values beyond its exchange-value. The operation of the market hides all this behind the facade of a simple exchange of equivalents by free, equal individuals.

Unlike in feudalism, the extraction of surplus-value under capitalism is hidden from all parties in the exchange because *it is automatic* once a capitalist productive process is established. The *direct* use of force is unnecessary for the extraction of surplus-labor as it is part and parcel of the capitalist relations of production, into which 'free' laborers must enter regardless of their will.

> The dull compulsion of economic relations completes the subjection of the laborer to the capitalist. Direct force, outside economic conditions, is of course still used, but only exceptionally. In the ordinary run of things, the laborer can be left to the "natural laws of production", i.e. to his dependence on capital, a dependence springing from, and guaranteed in perpetuity by, the conditions of production themselves.[11]

"Other than economic pressure" is unnecessary and the only role of the state in extraction of the surplus is maintenance of "the general external conditions of the capitalist mode of production against encroachment either by the workers or by individual capitalists."[12] That is, the state need only maintain a congenial juridical structure and protection from external attack.

Herein lies the primary basis for the separation of the state and economy in the capitalist mode of production. It is this concealed nature of the capitalist relations of production which make the state and production autonomous, or at least establishes the *possibility* of autonomy. There are other forces which make this separation *necessary*: the specific constitution of 'classes' which will be explored in the next chapter.

One issue must be raised here to counter possible criticism of this analysis. Because the capitalist accumulates surplus-value, at some point he or she has extracted enough to replace the original investment for the purchase of labor-power. From then on, the fund out of which the capitalist pays the workers is constituted by their past unpaid labor. Therefore one could argue, as did Marx, that no 'exchange' really takes place. The workers are merely returned a part of that which was originally 'stolen' from them; the capitalist exchanges nothing of her or his own.

Although this is in fact the case, it would be misleading to focus on it for our purposes. Exchange takes place regardless of whether the capitalist gives something of her or his own, or something which she or he has illicitly acquired previously. Exchange relations between workers and capitalists are real structures of capitalist societies with important effects on the relation between state and economy, on *intra*-class structure, and on the manner in which participants view their relations. The exchange relationship provides the foundation for the structure of the capitalist state and is a *real* activity of workers and capitalists. For the topic at hand it is irrelevant that, on a deeper level, the exchange is only apparent.

The elimination of force from the extraction of surplus labor under capitalism has several consequences. First, the disappearance of the necessity for force and the dissolution of the identical 'political/economic' relations of feudalism is the creation of 'private property' in a precise sense. In previous modes the productive process is mediated by the community and forms the main basis of community.[13] Under capitalism, community is dissolved because production rests on individualized exchange relations of the market. Production is regulated by the 'unintended effects' of this 'alienated community', i.e. the market.

When the community is excluded from regulating production, what emerges is:

> pure private property, which has cast off any semblance of a communal institution and has shut out the state from any influence on the development of property. To this modern private property corresponds the modern state ...[14]

Compared to other epochs, the res publica is severely restricted under capitalism.[15]

Secondly, the elimination of force from production *concentrates* the exercise of force in the institution of the state. This is the origin of the Weberian definition of the state as the "monopoly of the legitimate use of physical force within a given territory."[16] Here is the basis in capitalist relations of production of the liberal conception of the state as primarily an instrument of coercion, and for the origin of interpretations of the transcendence of the state (Marxian and non-Marxian alike) as the disappearance of coercion.[17]

Thirdly, and very importantly, the elimination of force from production establishes production as a separate, autonomous sphere, designated as the 'economy'. Economic laws and the comprehension of those laws ('economics') are only possible when production is separated from 'politics'. Although the 'economy' begins to be a possible, independent subject with the exchange of commodities between communities (as noted by Engels),[18] 'economics' cannot be developed as a discipline until the commodity form is generalized, i.e. until a fully developed exchange society exists. Evgeny B. Pashukanis argued this at length in *Law and Marxism*:

the economy only begins to be differentiated as a distinct sphere of relations with the emergence of exchange. So long as there are no relations determined by value, it is difficult to distinguish economic activity from the remaining totality of life's activities together with which it forms a synthetic whole. Pure natural economy cannot form the subject matter of political economy as an autonomous science. The relations of capitalist commodity production alone form the subject matter of political economy as an independent theoretical discipline employing its own concepts.[19]

The development of production as a separate sphere is the creation of the 'economy', 'economic laws', and 'economics'. Conversely, the abolition of the autonomy of production is the abolition of 'economics' because it is the abolition of economic laws on which an autonomous discipline could be constructed.

This argument is necessary to refute Engels' restatement of Saint-Simon's "politics is the science of production" as "the complete absorption of politics in economics."[20] Although intended to clarify the theory of the transcendence of the state, this phrase is terribly misleading because it does not acknowledge the dialectical relation between the emergence of a separate state and the autonomy of production. The 'economy' has no existence prior to, or separate from, capitalist production. The 'economy' is one of its particular products. Rather, the transcendence of the state is at the same time the overcoming of the 'economy', i.e. as Shlomo Avineri says, the "aufhebung" of the separation itself and the establishment of a new unity, a modern simultaneity of 'political' and 'economic' relations.[21]

This analysis also reveals a problem in Marx's formulation of the separation of politics and production under capitalism. If the 'economic' is only constituted by the dissolution of feudal relations of production, then it was a logical error of Marx to speak of "other than economic pressure" in the passage cited in the beginning of this chapter. To use the concept 'economic' rather than 'production' in reference to any age other than capitalism is to presuppose a separation that did not exist.[22] The terminology used in this discussion must be precise in order to avoid the ahistorical 'economic determinism' that characterized earlier Marxian and anti-Marxian accounts of the transcendence of the state and also in order to fully appreciate the break that existing socialist societies have made and the possibilities they have initiated.

To conceive of the 'economic' as a transhistorical existent is to forego one of the most powerful arguments for Marx's theory of the transcendence of the state: that the state is an historical product. The state does not exist throughout history, therefore there must be specific conditions which establish it. The task is to discover those conditions in the particular structure of production (the 'economic') under capitalism and evaluate the possibility of altering them.

If one assumes that the 'economic' is an eternal reality then the only possibility for the transcendence of the state is the development of a self-regulating (harmonious) productive process. We must consider the transcendence of the state and the transcendence of the economic as simultaneous in order to imagine an alternative manner of organizing society that comprises both. All other paths lead to attempts to improve the 'harmony' of the existing economic process, a project that Marx considered futile and referred to as "petty bourgeois reformism".

The foundation of the independent 'state' lies in the autonomy of production. This results from the establishment of production relations in the form of exchange relations between private owners of the factors of production. In contrast, Lenin acutely defined socialism as:

> the fight to break with the rotten past, which taught the people to regard the procurement of bread and clothes as a private affair, and buying and selling as a transaction 'which only concerns myself' -- [this] is a fight of world-historical significance, a fight between socialist consciousness and bourgeois-anarchist spontaneity.[23]

'Socialism' is the name given to the transition to the complete overcoming of the autonomy of state and economy. Socialism is the first step and provides the basis for the complete unification of previously separated 'state functions' and the 'economy'. Foremost it is the expansion of the res publica, the assertion of human collective control over production under modern conditions.[24] Only by conceiving the transcendence of the state as the overcoming of the autonomy of production can we see how central the transcendence of the state is to Marx's vision of communism.

1. Marx, *Capital* Volume 3 (New York: International Publishers, 1974), p. 791.

2. Nicos Poulantzas discusses these passages in *Political Power and Social Classes* (London: New Left Books, 1973), pp. 26-28.

3. Marx, *Capital* Volume 3, pp. 790-791.

4. Ibid., p. 790.

5. Ibid., p. 791.

6. Marx, *Capital* Volume 1 (New York: International Publishers, 1974), pp. 718-719.

7. Ibid., p. 714.

8. Ibid., p. 715.

9. Ibid., p. 714. See also ibid., p. 737.

10. Ibid., pp. 192-193.

11. Ibid., p. 737. See also Robin Blackburn, "Marxism: Theory of Proletarian Revolution," in *Revolution and Class Struggle: A Reader in Marxist Politics* (Glascow: Fontana and Collins, 1977), p. 41.

12. Engels, *Herr Eugen Duehring's Revolution in Science* [*Anti-Duehring*] (New York: International Publishers, 1976), p. 304.

13. Marx, *Grundrisse*, translated and introduced by Martin Nicolaus (New York: Vintage Books, 1973), pp. 475-476 and passim.

14. Marx and Engels, "The German Ideology," in *Marx-Engels Collected Works* Volume 5 (New York: International Publishers, 1976), pp. 89-90. See also ibid., p. 358.

90

15. See Nancy L. Schwartz, "Distinction Between Public and Private Life: Marx on the *zoon politikon*," *Political Theory* Volume 7, Number 2 (May 1979), pp. 245-266.

16. Max Weber, "Politics as a Vocation," in *From Max Weber: Essays in Sociology*, edited by H.H. Gerth and C. Wright Mills (New York: Oxford University Press/Galaxy Book, 1958), p. 78.

17. On the same page Weber favorably mentions Trotsky's opinion that "Every state is founded on force." Ibid., p. 78.

18. See Engels' discussion of this in his review [1859] of Marx's *A Contribution to the Critique of Political Economy*. Reprinted as an appendix to Karl Marx, ibid. (New York: International Publishers, 1976), p. 226. See also Evgeny B. Pashukanis' keen analysis of this issue in *Law and Marxism: A General Theory* (London: Ink Links, 1978), p. 57.

19. Pashukanis, op. cit., p. 57.

20. Engels, *Anti-Duehring*, p. 283.

21. Shlomo Avineri, *The Social and Political Thought of Karl Marx* (London: Cambridge University Press, 1968), pp. 202-203.

22. Ernesto Laclau, "The Specificity of the Political," in *Politics and Ideology in Marxist Theory* [three lengthy essays by Laclau] (London: New Left Books, 1977), pp. 73-77.

23. V. I. Lenin, "The Immediate Tasks of the Soviet Government" [April 28, 1918], in *Selected Works in Three Volumes* Volume 2 (New York: International Publishers, 1967), p. 660.

24. Etienne Balibar, *On the Dictatorship of the Proletariat* (London: New Left Books, 1977), pp. 152-153.

Chapter 6
Exchange Relations, Individuals, and 'Classes'

According to Marx, the possibility of the separation of state and society is established by the specific mode of extraction of surplus labor under capitalism. However, this separation only becomes *necessary* because of the specific constitution of classes under capitalism. Beginning with "On the Jewish Question" Marx argued consistently that the fragmentation of a division of labor mediated by exchange, i.e. the structure of the sphere of circulation, engenders a need for an independent institution embodying unity and community. Marx soon realized that these exchange relations are also the particular conditions of existence of classes under capitalism so that capitalist exploitation, exchange relations, and 'classes' in the precise sense of the term are (1) all intertwined with each other and (2) all contribute to the separation of state and society.

The separation of the majority from the means of production and the destruction of feudal-corporate forms, which bound everyone in limited communities, established labor as a commodity. The conditions of the bourgeois class were *generalized* by making everyone an 'owner' of a factor of production. These 'owners' are related in their social production by exchange; the market mediates among the various commodity owners.

This particular division of labor, i.e. the emergence of the "naked individual" confronting similar individuals in the market, is distinctive to capitalism. Production is fully 'social' because all producers depend on one another, on their exchange, for the satisfaction of their needs. Capitalism thereby creates the most intense interdependence of producers in an estranged form. Although production is recognized as interdependent and this interdependence yields a common interest, the latter interest is not an immediate determinant of the individual's actions. As Marx noted,

> the common interest which appears as a motive of the act as a whole is recognized as a fact by both sides; but, as such, it is not the motive, but rather procedes, as it were, behind the back of these self-reflected particular interests, behind the back of one individual's interest in opposition to that of the other.[1]

Or as Marx summed it up, "social production exists outside them as their fate."[2]

Instead of directly *social* production, money serves as the connection between individuals/owners; a social relation is thus mediated by a 'thing'.[3] The dissolution of previous communities and the extension of monetary relations proceeds simultaneously as more and more individuals are stripped of independent means of production and forced by circumstance to transform their activity, labor, into a commodity. Marx said succinctly of the relations of this fully developed exchange society, "the individual carries his social power, as well as his bond with society, in his pocket."[4]

From the early works on, Marx often noted this isolation and "atomization" of workers under capitalism. However, as he pointed out, properly speaking they are not "atoms", i.e. self-enclosed units. Individuals must enter relations with each other because of their needs.[5] Yet their needs are not "metabolized" consciously by a community; they are mediated in isolation by the uncontrolled market.

This development of 'free' individuality is extremely important for comprehending the basis and nature of the capitalist state, particularly in its ideological effects. As Rosa Luxemburg once noted, no one is juridically assigned a class position under capitalism. Individuals face each other in the market as owners, with equal rights and able to buy, sell, or do neither, as they will. This is also a 'just' system in that equivalent values are exchanged. Indeed, as Marx said, the market is "a very Eden of the innate rights of man."[6] The 'free' laborer is free in that her or his conditions of life are not imposed on her or him as under feudalism. In this situation, a person's position and relation to the means of production appear to be purely "accidental".[7]

Of course for Marx this freedom is an illusion. Society is not free; individuals are more *fully* bound to their class position when they are not assigned a position but are simply confronted by "material forces".

> The contradiction between the *democratic representative state* and *civil society* is the completion of the *classic* contradiction between public *commonweal* and *slavery*. In the modern world each person is *at the same time* a member of slave society and of the public commonweal. Precisely the *slavery of civil society* is *in appearance* the greatest *freedom* because it is in appearance the fully developed *independence* of the individual who considers as his *own* freedom the

uncurbed movement, no longer bound by a common bond or by man, of the estranged elements of his life, such as property, industry, religion, etc. whereas actually this is his fully developed slavery and inhumanity.[8]

For Marx the juridical freedom of individuals is a mask for their complete subjection to the material conditions of capitalist production.

Many Marxian theorists are content to point out the falsity of this conception of 'free, equal individuals' by showing that the real relations of power between different individuals are inscribed in the productive process of capitalism. However, Pashukanis and others have noted that this development is not *merely* 'ideological':

> The principle of legal subjectivity (which we take to mean the formal principle of freedom and equality, the autonomy of the personality, and so forth) is not only an instrument of deceit and a product of the hypocrisy of the bourgeoisie, insofar as it is used to counter the proletarian struggle to abolish classes, but is at the same time a concretely effective principle which is embodied in bourgeois society from the moment it emerges from and destroys feudal-patriarchical society. ... the victory of this principle is not only and not so much an ideological process (that is to say a process belonging entirely to the history of ideas, persuasions, and so on), but rather is an actual process, making human relations into legal relations, which accompanies the development of the economy based on the commodity and on money ...[9]

The development of the isolated individual in exchange, or "legal subjectivity", is a *real* process of social interaction. It is not merely an idea, subjectively held, but a concrete construction with tangible results such as contracts, law courts, and prisons.

That which Pashukanis asserted about the reality of legal individuality can be extended to the isolation of the individual by the capitalist division of labor, exchange relations, and the subsequent ideology of 'freedom and equality'. It is not merely 'ideology'; that is, this ideology has real, structural effects. As Poulantzas stated, the isolation of the individual in capitalism is "terrifyingly real".[10]

The modern state is grounded in the actuality of this isolation. The dissolution of communities into a 'society' of individuals and the development of the modern state are simultaneous, as Marx recognized in 1843.

> The *constitution* of the *political state* and the dissolution of civil society into independent *individuals* -- who are related by *law* as men in the estates and guilds are related by privilege -- are achieved in *one and the same act.*[11]

Fragmentation of community into individuals and unification by the state are two sides of the same process; in Poulantzas' phrase, it is a "dual movement".[12] The modern state emerges as the sole, immediate unification of individuals isolated by capitalist relations of production. Community is constituted above, and apart from, isolating social relations and, because of the equality of individuals, the state is the *universal* representative,tivetive ruling through universally applicable laws.

The important point is that under capitalist conditions of production in which the majority are deprived of independent means of production, everyone becomes a commodity-owner, if only of labor-power. However, the social production of these individuals is not directly regulated *as social* production but is mediated by exchange relations. Therefore individuals are isolated from one another, providing the basis for an institution which unifies them as 'people/nation'. This institution Marx called the "representative state", 'representative' in that it stands apart from and above other social relations, acting for the whole.

> The representative system is a very specific product of modern bourgeois society which is as inseparable from the latter as is the isolated individual of modern times.[13]

The representative state is simply the "practical-idealistic expression" of capitalist society.[14]

Because the state constitutes the unity of the represented, it must be essentially free and independent. As Thomas Hobbes (one of Marx's favorite philosophers) argued well about the modern state, the 'people' do not have a unity apart from the state; the state creates community. In order for the state to perform this function, it must be institutionally separated from, and superior to, society. Marx corrected Hobbes by insisting that the state does not create community ex nihilo: there is a substratum of (albeit alienated)

interdependence resulting from the fact that production is *social* production; we are not 'Crusoes'. Nonetheless the state's major function is that of
unifying the capitalist social formation and this makes it autonomous and
superior to other social relations, producing it as a separate institution. The
state emerges as the sole embodiment of community.

The real force behind the maintenance of these isolating conditions of
production, and therefore the state, is that the exchange relations which engender the state are also the specific conditions of existence of the dominant
class in capitalism and necessary for its specific mode of extraction of
surplus-labor. Because of the difference between the exchange-value and
use-value of labor-power, *exchange itself* constitutes the specific form of
capitalist exploitation. The exchange relation is both necessary to and veils
the existence of exploitation and class relations and maintenance of this individual exchange society is at the same time maintenance of the economic
rule of the bourgeoisie. Exchange is the primary condition of existence of
the bourgeois class. Consequently, exchange relations between capital and
labor *and* within the bourgeoisie itself define the 'bourgeoisie' just as much
as 'ownership of the means of production' does. The bourgeoisie cannot be
adequately comprehended by mere reference to the sphere of production
but must also be defined by its specific conditions of existence in the sphere
of circulation.

As Marx argued in *The German Ideology*, the conditions of existence of
the bourgeoisie in individualized exchange relations necessarily fragment
the class. Not only are members of the bourgeoisie isolated from one another
like all individuals under capitalism, but they face each other as hostile com-
petitors. Marx further asserted in *The German Ideology* and other places
that this 'ontological' fragmentation of the bourgeoisie necessitates a state
to maintain the general conditions of capitalist exploitation, a thesis which
Nicos Poulantzas argued as the state's "organizational role vis-a-vis the
dominant class."[15]

In *The Manifesto of the Communist Party* Marx said that the state serves the "whole bourgeoisie".[16] Engels made this even clearer by his previously cited remark that the state must preserve the capitalist relations of
production "against encroachments either by the workers or by individual
capitalists."[17] In order for the state to perform its unifying function it must
have autonomy from this or that individual bourgeois. The state has independence because of the internal structure of the bourgeois class, not *at its*

behest. The state is not the instrument of a pre-constituted bourgeoisie, i.e. the 'tool' of a class subject. The state is an objective structure resulting from the capitalist mode of production and the specific internal structure of the bourgeoisie; it is not dependent on a 'class will'. Contrary to a common interpretation, the bourgeoisie is *forged* into a class subject, develops a 'class will', only *through* the representation of the state. It is the 'class conditions' of the bourgeoisie which produce the state, not the bourgeoisie acting *as a class.*

The state serves as a kind of arena for the formulation of a common prgramme for the bourgeoisie as a whole. For this reason Marx and Lenin often referred to the "republic" as the best form for the constitution of the 'class will' of the bourgeoisie.[18] France, with its fiercely antagonistic bourgeois fractions was only a clear example of what Marx considered to be the rule for all of Europe: the republic is necessary for the rule of bourgeoisie as a *class.*[19]

> [I]t is precisely the interests of the bourgeoisie, the material conditions of its class rule and class exploitation, which form the substance of the bourgeois republic.[20]

We can also understand civil liberties in this light. In order for the bourgeoisie to reach a consensus on a common programme, public discussion is necessary and so are the traditional freedoms associated with democratic republics.

However we must not take this discussion as absolute. Marx was fairly cynical with regard to civil liberties, generally considering them instruments of the bourgeoisie in their struggle for power and concretely interpreted in such a way as to keep others from power.[21] We must also not forget Engels' remark in a letter that "Bonapartism is after all the real religion of the modern bourgeoisie."[22] Although 'Bonapartism', 'Bismarckism', 'Caesarism', and 'fascism' are often referred to as "exceptional regimes" in Marxian literature, thereby implying that the 'republic' is the normal state for capitalism, this identification has been recently challenged in a study of capitalism and democracy in Latin America.[23] We cannot further explore this issue here so suffice it to say that the modern state must be constructed in some way such that it can perform the role of 'arena' for the formulation of a common programme for the bourgeoisie. The *necessary* and *universal* condition for this is that the state be constituted as a separate sphere, independent and superior to other social relations.

In sum, the conditions of existence of the bourgeoisie are essentially fragmenting, necessitating a representative state to forge unity and secure the economic rule of the class as a *whole*. Only by comprehending this can we see why the bourgeoisie 'expresses' itself in the mediated form of the representative state rather than ruling directly in a feudal or absolute manner.[24]

The ability of the bourgeoisie to extract surplus labor through the exchange process itself (given the separation of the majority from independent means of production) makes the autonomy of the state possible. The independence of the state is only made *necessary* by (1) the isolating effects of exchange relations, the conditions of bourgeois exploitation, on individuals, (2) the intra-class competition of the bourgeoisie, requiring a forum within which to formulate a common policy, and (3) the need for a structure to enforce the general interest of the class against the individual's particular interests and actions. The bourgeoisie does not exist as a pre-constituted historical subject; its organization as a class depends on the establishment of an institution that unifies it and, therefore, stands in a representative relation to it.

In the discussion of this point in *The German Ideology* the question was raised whether the proletariat, a class in the precise sense like the bourgeoisie, would not *also* require political representation to act on its class interests. Marx's answer to this question contains one of his most important arguments for the real possibility of the transcendence of the state.

Although the proletariat is a 'class', Marx believed that the proletariat escapes the need for political representation, that the movement of the proletariat to historical subjectivity is essentially unproblematic. One could even call this the 'political secret' of the proletariat.

One of the reasons the proletariat can forego political representation is the tendency of capitalism to simplify social relations. As Marx and Engels noted in various early works, capitalism dissolves all traditional structures into monetary relations, i.e. the 'cash nexus'.

> The bourgeoisie, wherever it has got the upper hand, has put an end
> to all feudal, idyllic relations. It has pitilessly torn asunder the mot-

ley feudal ties that bound man to his 'natural superiors', and has left
no other nexus between man and man than naked self-interest, than
callous 'cash payment'.[25]

Barriers between town and country are abolished with the transformation
of landowners into agricultural capitalists and peasants into an agricultural
proletariat.[26] Finally, these capitalist relations are generalized over the
globe, destroying "the peculiar features of various nationalities."[27] As Marx
concluded, if nothing else, modern industry is a "leveler".[28]

Along with the simplification of social relations between classes is the
simplification of the *intra*-class structure specifically of the proletariat.
Marx argued that capitalism reduces the need for skilled labor by introduc-
ing machinery. According to Marx, "skilled labor" properly speaking only
belongs to the period of "manufacture".

> Along with the tool, the skill of the workman in handling it passes
> over to the machine. The capabilities of the tool are emancipated from
> the restraints that are inseparable from human labor-power. Thereby
> the technical foundation on which is based the division of labor in
> manufacture is swept away. Hence, in the place of the hierarchy of
> specialized workmen that characterizes manufacture, there steps, in
> the automatic factory, a tendency to equalize and reduce to one and
> same level every kind of work that has to be done by the minders of
> the machines; in the place of the artificially produced differentiations
> of the detail workmen, step the natural differences of age and sex.[29]

With the development of 'industry' as opposed to 'manufacture', man becomes

> an appendage to the machine, and it is only the most simple, most
> monotonous, and most easily acquired knack, that is required of
> him.[30]

Equalization of skill level and conditions of labor unifies the proletariat,
homogenizes it, and "reduces wages to the same low level."[31] The fragmentation of interests resulting from the division of labor is lessened by the objective tendency of capitalism to obliterate the differentiated skill levels
upon which intra-class divisions are partially based. (It does not reduce the
intra-class competition at any particular skill level.)

Marx and Engels did frequently notice the persistence of skill differen-
ces in certain cases (especially England) which created a more conserva-
tive section of the proletariat, the "labor aristocracy".[32] However Marx and
Engels did not consider this to be a structural characteristic of capitalism
nor of the proletariat and did not believe that it would disrupt the historical
tendencies of capitalism.

The simplification of skill levels is accompanied by the concentration
of workers in large factories and in urban areas.[33] This concentration makes
it possible for workers to combine more easily: the working class is "disciplined, united, organized by the very mechanism of the process of
capitalism itself."[34]

Marx distinguished this unique characteristic of the proletariat as a class
by contrasting it with the other exploited class in European society, the
peasantry, especially in his discussions of the regime of Napoleon III.
Peasants are culturally isolated; they live in the same situation as each other
but their class conditions do not create "manifold relationships" among
them. Their production is primarily self-sufficient, therefore 'society' is
marginal to their lives.

> Thus the great mass of the French nation is formed by the simple ad-
> dition of isomorphous magnitudes, much as potatoes in a sack form
> a sack of potatoes. In so far as millions of families live under
> economic conditions of existence that separate their mode of life,
> their interests and their cultural formation from those of other clas-
> ses and bring them into conflict with those classes, they form a class.
> In so far as these small peasant proprietors are merely connected on
> a local basis, and the identity of their interests fails to produce a feel-
> ing of community, national links, or a political organization, they do
> not form a class. They are therefore incapable of asserting their class
> interest in their own name ... They cannot represent themselves; they
> must be represented.[35]

Their representative was Napoleon III, whom they elected through universal suffrage. In this way the French peasantry served as the "passive
economical basis" of the Second Empire.[36]

It is this "rural idiocy" of the peasants ('idiocy' in the sense of 'isolation'
-- as in 'idiom' -- not 'stupidity')[37] that makes the proletariat the only class
capable of making the revolution against capitalism. The position of the
proletariat in production, unlike the peasantry, allows it to escape this neces-

sity for political representation and places it in a unique position of being able to turn the "existing conditions into conditions of unity."[38]

The general simplification of social relations under capitalism, the ever-increasing homogeneity of the proletariat, and the particular role of the proletariat in the capitalist mode of production all result in making the proletariat an epistemologically privileged class. Marx repeatedly stressed the automatic growth of class consciousness of the proletariat. According to Engels, Marx always "entirely trusted to the intellectual development of the working class, which was sure to result from combined action and mutual discussion."[39] "And," Engels added, "Marx was right."

Consequently, Marx argued that the communist parties have no independent organizational function in regard to the proletarian movement. "Communist consciousness" will be achieved without the mediation of a political party in a modern sense.[40] As Marx phrased it, "communism" is not an "invention" but the "expression" of an existing historical movement.[41]

The idea that the proletariat can achieve revolutionary consciousness on its own is central to the distinction between Marx's communism (as he conceived it) and earlier utopian thought. In a rather lengthy passage in *The Poverty of Philosophy* Marx explained the distinction and developed the position he was always to maintain.

> Just as the *economists* are the scientific representatives of the bourgeois class, so the *Socialists* and the *Communists* are the theoreticians of the proletarian class. So long as the proletariat is not sufficiently developed to constitute itself as a class, and consequently so long as the struggle itself of the proletariat with the bourgeoisie has not yet assumed a political character, and the productive forces are not yet sufficiently developed in the bosom of the bourgeoisie itself to enable us to catch a glimpse of the material conditions necessary for the emancipation of the proletariat and for the formation of a new society, these theoreticians are merely utopians who, to meet the wants of the oppressed classes, improvise systems and go in search of a regenerating science. But in the measure that history moves forward, and with it the struggle of the proletariat assumes clearer outlines, they no longer need to seek science in their minds; they have only to take note of what is happening before their eyes and *to become its mouthpiece.* [my emphasis] So long as they look for science and merely make systems, so long as they are at the beginning of the struggle, they see in

poverty nothing but poverty, without seeing in it the revolutionary, subversive side, which will overthrow the old society. From this moment, science, which is a product of the historical movement, has associated itself consciously with it, has ceased to be doctrinaire and has become revolutionary.[42]

Marx always explained utopianism and system-building as the response to an underdeveloped period, the early period of the proletariat. As such, utopian socialists stand in the same relation to communists as "alchemists" to modern chemistry.[43] Although the communists do not repudiate these "oracles of social science", the real movement can now determine its own course.[44]

Marx could propose this relationship between communists and the workers' movement because he believed that one of the consequences of the simplification and clarification of social relations is that the working class is *inescapably* revolutionary.

It is not a question of what this or that proletarian, or even the whole proletariat, at the moment *regards* as its aim. It is a question of *what the proletariat is*, and what, in accordance with this *being*, it will historically be compelled to do.[45]

Although there will be lulls in the revolutionary storm (e.g. after 1848),[46] the age as a whole is necessarily revolutionary. Part of the very definition of the proletariat is precisely its revolutionary character: "the working class is revolutionary or it is nothing ..."[47]

As with Lenin, one of the keys to Marx's thought is what Lukacs called an insistence on the "actuality of the revolution." Marx's philosophical position, as well as his social analysis, convinced him that this age is necessarily revolutionary. As Lukacs said succinctly:

For historical materialism as the conceptual expression of the proletariat's struggle for liberation could only be conceived and formulated theoretically when revolution was already on the historical agenda as a practical reality ...[48]

This is of course an echo of Marx's well-known theses that "revolutionary ideas presuppose the existence of a revolutionary class"[49] and "mankind inevitably sets itself only such tasks as it is able to solve" (a favorite of Antonio Gramsci).[50] This belief also underscores Marx's insistence on the separation of workers' organizations from others, regardless of short-term losses.[51] At times this belief produced an almost fatalistic attitude toward the revolution, as in this passage from Engels.

> [T]he revolution does not allow conditions to be dictated to it. Either one is a revolutionary and accepts the consequences of the revolution, whatever they may be, or one is thrown into the arms of the counter-revolution ...[52]

Six months after this was written Engels was in combat in Germany.

This assurance of the "actuality of the revolution" gave Marx and Engels a specific conception of the *political* dimension of the struggle. Against all "sects", "dictators of the working class" (i.e. Lasalle), and bourgeois reformers, Marx insisted that "the emancipation of the working classes must be conquered by the working classes themselves."[53] He frequently counterposed "sectarianism" to the "spontaneous organization of the working class."[54] "Doctrinaire recipes" would only restrict the working class movement;[55] their time had passed when the proletariat became a "free, autonomous, historical movement."[56]

One of the most stunning examples of the defense of his principle of freedom of the working class movement from "enlightened guidance" is the "Circular Letter to Bebel, Liebknecht, Bracke, et al.," to the leadership of the German Social-Democratic Workers' Party.[57] In response to workers' parliamentary deputies voting contrary to the party platform and their weak justification that it is necessary to entrust parliamentary issues to the deputies because "the simple worker" doesn't have the leisure to comprehend such issues, Marx and Engels simply said, "So vote bourgeois!"[58] They went on to remind the leadership of what Marx and Engels believed to be the first principles of the movement.

> When the International was formed, we expressly formulated the battle-cry: the emancipation of the working class must be the work of the working class itself. We cannot ally ourselves, therefore, with people who openly declare that the workers are too uneducated to free themselves and must be liberated from above by philanthropic big bourgeois and petty bourgeois.[59]

It is no surprise that Marx had such a strong reaction to Bakunin's charge that Marx aimed at a post-revolutionary, educated elite.[60]

The idea that a communist organization should structure the workers' movement was always scorned by Marx, whether it came from "philanthropic big bourgeois" or from the 'left'. Marx firmly believed that Bakunin and his Alliance for Socialist Democracy aimed at precisely such structuring.

> To them, the working class is so much raw material, a chaos which needs the breath of their Holy Spirit to give it form.[61]

According to Hal Draper it is precisely this profound belief that the workers will emancipate themselves that distinguishes Marx's conception of revolution from all that preceded it. Earlier socialists had only viewed the working class as a poverty-ridden class to be helped, as at most the 'shock troops' of the revolution.[62] This always raises the question, as Marx did in the third of his "Theses on Feuerbach," of who is to "educate the educator."[63] Instead Marx proposed the possibility of the "self-emancipation" of the working class and was opposed to what Draper, following certain hints by Marx and Engels, calls "octroyal socialism", i.e. socialism 'given' to the working class by some 'higher authority'.[64]

> Marxism, as the theory and practice of proletarian revolution, therefore also had to be the theory and practice of the self-emancipation of the proletariat. *Its essential originality flows from this source.*[65]

Socialism given from above, like the democracy presented by the King of Prussia and Bismarck, is by that very fact emasculated.

The 'simplification' and 'clarification' theses and the idea of the 'self-emancipation' of the working class severely circumscribe the role of political organizations of the working class in Marx's theory. Marx was quite explicit about this in discussing the origin and limits of the International.

> It is the business of the International Working Men's Association to combine and generalize the *spontaneous movements* of the working classes, but not to dictate or impose any doctrinaire system whatsoever.[66]

This follows from Marx's conception of the International as "the spontaneous growth of the proletarian movement."[67] It is also in accordance with the role of the communist 'party' outlined in the *Manifesto* two decades earlier.[68]

104

The International did have several functions, all of which come down to the voluntary education and unification of action of the working class. It was essentially a forum for discussion by the different national proletariats and tendencies.

> Since the sections of the working class in various countries have reached different stages of development, it follows that their theoretical opinions, which reflect the real movement, will be equally divergent.[69]

By fostering discussion the International "cannot fail gradually to give rise to a common theoretical program."[70]

The main problem of the International was to combat two, often intertwined sources of disruption: intra-class competition and national rivalries. Marx and Engels were very much aware of the reality of competition of workers against workers and of the importance of limiting it. Marx keenly analyzed the tensions between English and Irish proletarians in England and their effects on the workers' movement.

> *This antagonism* is the *secret of the impotence of the English working class*, despite its organization. It is the secret which enables the capitalist class to maintain its power, as this class is perfectly aware.[71]

Marx concluded that the chief problems of the English proletarian revolution originated in Ireland and that that is where the first blow would have to be struck.[72]

Of course there were also national distinctions created by the position of respective countries in the international market. In a despairing letter to Marx in 1858 Engels wrote:

> the English proletariat is actually becoming more and more bourgeois, so that this most bourgeois of all nations is apparently aiming at the possession of a bourgeois aristocracy and a bourgeois proletariat *alongside* the bourgeoisie. For a nation which exploits the whole world this is of course to a certain extent justifiable.[73]

This was difficult for the International to grapple with and, unfortunately, Marx and Engels did not further analyze this structural contradiction within the international proletariat.[74] In any case they expected that the favorable position of the English working class would decline as capitalist relations were firmly established in other countries.

Marx's view of the proletariat as an essentially self-constituting. self-emancipating historical subject led him to consistently undervalue the need for a political 'party' in any important sense. It should be recalled that the word 'party' itself did not have its modern meaning. It was closer to the modern word 'movement' than concrete political organization.[75] This indicates one of the key sources of Marx's optimism in regard to the possibility of transcending the state.

This point was brought out perfectly by the Italian Marxist Rossana Rossanda. According to Rossanda, Marx's idea of revolution is 'immediate'; it does not allow for a separate role of a political party in the modern sense. Marx always argued that the course of the revolution is determined by the practical tasks that the proletariat faces in carrying it out.[76] This conception of revolution does not allow a previous plan,

> a design which anticipates the ongoing material circumstances, ... [and] a consciousness of history and of class which antedate both, and which are exterior to and separate from them.[77]

Marx's conception of revolution as determined by immediate circumstances -- "enemies to be struck down, measures to be taken" -- precludes a major reason for a political party in a modern sense.[78]

Marx believed proletarian political action to be a mere "expression" of a preconstituted, historical subject. Rossanda connected Marx's rejection of an independent political organization of the proletariat (i.e. 'independent' of the *proletariat*) with his view of the Paris Commune of 1871 and the unproblematic nature of its institutions.

> It is not by chance that the proletariat is destined to destroy and over-come the traditional modes of political expression, including its own, insofar as they are something else than direct social rule; and it achieves this by that unique form of revolution and of a revolutionary society which Marx depicted: the Commune of 1871. ... direct democracy thus appeared not as an elementary form of proletarian power but as its *specific* form. In the model of the Commune, there-fore, the revolution and the revolutionary society anticipated not only the withering away of the state, but even more radically, the progres-sive disappearance of the *political* dimension as a dimension separate

from (and opposed to) social being, reconstituted in its unity. The proletariat in struggle does not produce an institution distinct from its immediate being; and no more does it produce its own state, distinct from the immediate being of the new society. If, that is to say, one does not find a theory of the party in Marx, the reason is that, in his theory of the revolution, there is neither need nor room for it.[79]

Marx's detailed characterization of the Paris Commune will be discussed in the next chapter. Suffice it to say here that the development of a conception of the party depends on a different analysis of the possibilities of the proletariat in its 'immediate being', i.e. it depended on Kautsky and Lenin.

Marx's conception of the simplification and clarification of social relations, the increasing homegeneity of the proletariat, and the necessarily revolutionary nature of the proletariat gave rise to a specific notion of the proletarian revolution itself. His predominant view is that of the proletariat as a self-constituting historical actor, its revolutionary course more or less governed by immediate circumstances and not producing any long-lasting political forms. Political form is not necessary for the substantial organization of the proletariat as a class. For this reason the "political dimension" is only a phenomenon of its struggle against other classes and 'politics' never achieves an existence apart from the proletariat itself; it is merely its "expression".

Although I have thus far only been concerned with the proletariat, Marx and Engels sometimes spoke as if *all* political struggles were simply the "expression" of various classes and class fractions. Engels established this identity in very clear terms in *The German Ideology*:

> all struggles within the state, the struggle between democracy, aristocracy, and monarchy, the struggle for the franchise, etc. etc., are merely the illusory forms -- altogether the general interest is the illusory form of the common interests -- in which the real struggles of the different classes are fought out among one another ...[80]

In a letter many years later (1890) Engels softened this view somewhat, as he did so many other views:

> the struggle between classes already existing and fighting with one another is reflected in the struggle between government and opposition, but likewise in inverted form, no longer directly but indirectly, not as a class struggle but as a fight for political principles, and is so

distorted that it has taken us thousands of years to get to the bottom of it.[81]

This is the basis of the innumerable instances of references to political actors as "expressions" of this or that class[82] and also the various descriptions of the state itself as "epitome of civil society",[83] "official resume of civil society",[84] and the many examples of "official expression".[85]

With regard to the bourgeoisie, the peasantry, and the aristocracy, the word "expression" is merely descriptive. Their political "expressions" take on an independent existence, and *must* do so in order for these groups to articulate themselves as political actors. Marx merely indicated the class content of certain phenomena in this case, rather than analyzed the actual relation between the social groups and their political organizations.

However, Marx believed that the proletariat is different. His predominant view of the proletariat is that it becomes organized *as a class* purely by virtue of its position in the capitalist relations of production. It needs political forms only in the immediate struggle with other classes. Unlike other classes, the political organizations of the proletariat do not take on an independent relation to the class. The party of the proletariat is purely an instrument wielded by the unified class-subject.

In this manner the proletariat escapes the dialectic of representation that entraps all other classes. Its political form is *merely* an "expression", a phenomenon depending on immediate circumstances of class struggle and having no basis for existence once the struggle subsides. The transcendence of the state is in this way inscribed in Marx's conception of the relation of the proletariat to its political form.

Herein also lies the much-noticed reservations Marx always had against clearly outlining communist society and the phases of its development, of which the transcendence of the state is a part. *Marx's conception of proletarian revolution precluded him from explicating in detail the process of development toward communism.* This process would be determined by the revolutionary movement itself. Any attempt to forecast this process would be purely utopian and contradict Marx's conception of the revolutionary process and his predominant conception of the proletariat. Like Lenin, Marx steadfastly refused to "write recipes for the cookshops of the future."

At this point the relation between Marx's understanding of the political needs (or lack thereof) of the proletariat and stateless society may appear quite abstract, more a 'theme' than a logical argument. The theme is that of the absence of the need for an independent political structure representing the proletariat. The relationship between this 'political secret' of the proletariat and the transcendence of the state is somewhat clarified by examining the specific formulations of the theory of the transcendence of the state as they emerged from various political battles of Marx and Engels and especially from Marx's analysis of the Paris Commune of 1871.

1. Marx, *Grundrisse*, translated and introduced by Martin Nicolaus (New York: Vintage Books, 1973), p. 244.

2. Ibid., p. 158.

3. Ibid., p. 239.

4. Ibid., p. 157.

5. Marx and Engels, *The Holy Family, or Critique of Critical Criticism* (Moscow: Progress Publishers, 1975), p. 142.

6. Marx, *Capital* Volume One (New York: International Publishers, 1974), p. 176. See also Marx, *Grundrisse*, p. 245.

7. Marx and Engels, "The German Ideology," in *Marx-Engels Collected Works* Volume 5 (New York: International Publishers, 1976), pp. 78-79.

8. Marx and Engels, *The Holy Family*, p. 137.

9. Evgeny B. Pashukanis, *Law and Marxism: A General Theory* (London: Ink Links, 1978), p. 40.

10. Nicos Poulantzas, *Political Power and Social Classes* (London: New Left Books, 1973), p. 130. See also Poulantzas, *State, Power, Socialism* (London: New Left Books/Verso, 1978), pp. 69-70.

11. Marx, "On the Jewish Question," in *Karl Marx: Early Writings*, introduced by Lucio Colletti (New York: Vintage Books, 1975), p. 233.

12. Poulantzas, *State, Power, Socialism*, p. 70.

13. Marx and Engels, "The German Ideology," p. 200.

14. Ibid., p. 52. For other comments on the intimate relation between the representative state and capitalism, see: Marx and Engels, *The Holy Family*, p. 135 and p. 144; Marx and Engels, "The Manifesto of the Communist

Party," in *The Revolutions of 1848: Political Writings Volume I*, edited and introduced by David Fernbach (New York: Random House, 1974), p. 69; Marx, "The Trial of the Rhineland District Committee of Democrats. Speech by Karl Marx in His Own Defense" [1849], in ibid., p. 251; Marx and Engels, "Reviews from the *Neue Rheinische Zeitung Revue*: May-October 1850," in ibid., p. 299; Marx, "The Chartists," in *Surveys From Exile: Political Writings Volume II*, edited and introduced by David Fernbach (New York: Random House, 1974), p. 263; and Engels, letter to Eduard Bernstein (March 24, 1884), in *Marx-Engels Selected Correspondence* (Moscow: Progress Publishers, 1975), p. 350.

15. Poulantzas, *State, Power, Socialism*, p. 32. See also, Poulantzas, *Political Power and Social Classes*, pp. 287-288.

16. Marx and Engels, "The Manifesto," p. 69.

17. Engels, *Herr Eugen Duehring's Revolution in Science* [*Anti-Duehring*] (New York: International Publishers, 1976), p. 304.

18. Marx, "The Bourgeoisie and the Counter-Revolution," in *The Revolutions of 1848*, pp. 189-190. See also Poulantzas, *State, Power, Socialism*, p. 32, and *Political Power and Social Classes*, pp. 287-288. Finally, see also footnote 14 above.

19. Marx, "The Class Struggles in France: 1848-1850," in *Surveys From Exile*, p. 89; see also Marx, "The Eighteenth Brumaire of Louis Bonaparte," in ibid., p. 215.

20. Marx, "The Class Struggles in France," pp. 63-64.

21. Ibid., p. 127; see also Marx, "The Eighteenth Brumaire of Louis Bonaparte," p. 159.

22. Engels, letter to Marx (April 13, 1866), in *Marx-Engels Selected Correspondence*, p. 166.

23. Atilio A. Boron, "Latin America: Between Hobbes and Friedman," *New Left Review* Number 130 (November-December 1981), pp. 45-46.

24. Pashukanis, op. cit., pp. 138-140.

25. Marx and Engels, "The Manifesto," p. 70. See also Marx and Engels, "The German Ideology," pp. 372-373; and Marx, *Grundrisse*, p. 410.

26. Marx, "The Trial of the Rhineland District Committee," p. 260.

27. Marx and Engels, "The German Ideology," pp. 72-73.

28. Marx, "The Trial of the Rhineland District Committee," p. 260. See also Marx, *Capital* Volume One, page 397.

29. Marx, *Capital* Volume One, p. 420. The last sentence refers to the practice of using women and children as skill levels were reduced. See also Marx and Engels, "The Manifesto," p. 75.

30. Marx and Engels, "The Manifesto," p. 74.

31. Ibid., p 75.

32. Marx and Engels, "Reviews from the *Neue Rheinische Zeitung Revue*," p. 308.

33. Marx, *Capital* Volume One, p. 503.

34. Ibid., p. 763.

35. Marx, "The Eighteenth Brumaire," pp. 238-239. See also Marx, "The First Draft of 'The Civil War in France'," in *The First International and After: Political Writings Volume III*, edited and introduced by David Fernbach (New York: Random House, 1974), pp. 256-257.

112

36. Marx, "The First Draft of 'The Civil War in France'," in *Writings on the Paris Commune (Marx-Engels)*, edited and introduced by Hal Draper (New York: Monthly Review Press, 1971), p. 151.

37. Marx and Engels, "The Manifesto," p. 71. Hal Draper has clarified this phrase by pointing out that there are *two* words in German that can be translated 'idiocy' but actually have very different meanings: 'Idiotismus' and 'Idiotie'. The former was used in Marx's passage -- "dem Idiotismus des Landlebens" -- and it specifically means 'isolation', not 'stupidity'. See Draper, *Karl Marx's Theory of Revolution Volume II: The Politics of Social Classes* (New York: Monthly Review Press, 1978), pp. 344-348. In all of his work Draper is an invaluable model of scholarship.

38. Marx and Engels, "The German Ideology," p. 81.

39. Engels, "Preface to the English Edition [of 'The Manifesto'] of 1888," in *The Revolutions of 1848*, p. 63.

40. Marx and Engels, "The German Ideology," p. 52.

41. Marx and Engels, "The Manifesto," p. 80. See also Marx and Engels, "The German Ideology," p. 49.

42. Marx, *The Poverty of Philosophy* (New York: International Publishers, 1973), pp. 125-126. See also Marx and Engels, "The Manifesto," pp. 95-96; and Marx "The Class Struggles in France," pp. 122-123.

43. Marx used this analogy twice: in "The Alleged Splits in the International" [1872], in *The First International and After*, p. 299; and in "Political Indifferentism" [1873], in ibid., p. 329.

44. Marx, "Political Indifferentism," p. 330.

45. Marx and Engels, *The Holy Family*, p. 44 and pp. 43-45.

46. Marx, "The Minutes of the Central Committee Meeting of September 15, 1850," in *The Revolutions of 1848*, p. 343. See also Marx, "The Eighteenth Brumaire," p. 194.

47. Marx, letter to Schweitzer (February 13, 1865), in *The First International and After*, p. 148. See also Marx, "Address of the Central Committee to the Communist League (March 1850)," in *The Revolutions of 1848*, p. 319. David Fernbach interprets this phrase somewhat differently in his introduction to *The First International and After*, p. 59.

48. Georg Lukacs, *Lenin: A Study on the Unity of His Thought* (Cambridge: The MIT Press, 1974), p. 11.

49. Marx and Engels, "The German Ideology," p. 60. 50. Marx, *A Contribution to the Critique of Political Economy* (New York: International Publishers, 1976), p. 21.

51. Marx, "Address of the Central Committee," p. 327 and p. 330.

52. Engels, "Democratic Pan-Slavism" [1849], in *The Revolutions of 1848*, p. 244.

53. Marx, "Provisional Rules [of the First International]," in *The First International and After*, p. 82.

54. Marx, "The General Council to the Federal Council of French Switzerland" [January 1870], in *The First International and After*, p. 120. See also Marx and Engels, "The Manifesto," p. 95.

55. Marx, letter to Schweitzer (October 13, 1868), in *The First International and After*, pp. 155-156.

56. Marx, "The Class Struggles in France," p. 122.

57. Marx, "Circular Letter to Bebel, Liebknecht, Bracke, et al." [September 17-18, 1879], in *The First International and After*, pp. 360-375. This ex-

114

tremely important document is only partly reproduced in *Marx-Engels Selected Correspondence*, pp. 302-307.

. Marx, "Circular Letter," p. 369.

59. Ibid., p. 375. Not surprisingly, Eduard Bernstein was one of the members of the 'Zurich Commission' against whom this letter was directed.

60. Marx, "Conspectus of Bakunin's *Statism and Anarchy*," in *The First International and After*, p. 337.

61. Marx, "The Alleged Splits in the International," p. 306.

62. Hal Draper, "The Principle of Self-Emancipation in Marx and Engels," in *The Socialist Register 1971*, edited by Ralph Miliband and John Saville (London: Merlin Press, 1971), p. 95.

63. Marx, "Theses on Feuerbach," in *Karl Marx: Early Writings*, p. 422.

64. Draper, "The Principle of Self-Emancipation," p. 101.

65. Ibid., p. 106. Draper always insists on the centrality of the notion of 'self- emancipation' for Marx, although later attributing the originality of the notion to William Thompson: see Hal Draper, *Karl Marx's Theory of Revolution Volume I, Book I: State and Bureaucracy* (New York: Monthly Review Press, 1977), p. 214. See also Draper, *Karl Marx's Theory of Revolution Volume II: The Politics of Social Classes*, p. 164.

66. Marx, "Instructions for Delegates to the Geneva Congress" [1866], in *The First International and After*, p. 90.

67. Marx, "Report to the Brussels Congress" [1868], in *The First International and After*, p. 99. See the similar argument in an early letter to Ruge: "Marx to Ruge (September 1843)," in *Karl Marx: Early Writings*, p, 207 and p. 209.

68. Marx and Engels, "The Manifesto," pp. 79-80.

69. Marx, "The Alleged Splits in the International," p. 280.

70. Ibid., p. 280.

71. Marx, letter to Meyer and Vogt (April 1870), in *The First International and After*, p. 169. See also Marx, "The General Council to the Federal Council of French Switzerland," in ibid., p. 117.

72. Marx, letter to Meyer and Vogt (April 1870), p. 167.

73. Engels, letter to Marx (October 7, 1858), in *Marx-Engels Selected Correspondence*, p. 103.

74. Ernest Mandel has engaged in such analyses of the present-day movement: e.g. *From Stalinism to Eurocommunism* (London: New Left Books, 1978).

75. David Fernbach, "Introduction" to *The Revolutions of 1848*, p. 28.

76. Marx, "The Class Struggles in France," p. 45.

77. Rossana Rossanda, "Class and Party," in *The Socialist Register 1970*, edited by Ralph Miliband and John Saville (London: Merlin Press 1970), p. 219.

78. Marx, "The Class Struggles in France," p. 45.

79. Rossanda, op. cit., p. 220.

80. Marx and Engels, "The German Ideology," pp. 46-47.

81. Engels, letter to Conrad Schmidt (October 27, 1890), *Marx-Engels Selected Correspondence*, p. 399.

82. Marx and Engels, "Reviews From the *Neue Rheinische Zeitung Revue*," p. 273; Marx, "The Eighteenth Brumaire," p. 173 and p. 189.

83.Marx and Engels, "The German Ideology," p. 90.

84. Marx, letter to P. V. Annckov (December 28, 1846), appended to *The Poverty of Philosophy*, p. 181.

85. Marx, "Critical Notes on 'The King of Prussia and Social Reform'," in *Karl Marx: Early Writings*, pp. 412-413. See also Marx and Engels, "The German Ideology," p. 52; and Marx, *The Poverty of Philosophy*, p. 122. The examples could easily be multiplied.

Chapter 7

Different Formulations of the Theory

Marx's theory of the transcendence of the state was born of his theoretical attack on Hegel and developed in the struggle of Marx and Engels against the ideas of the Left-Hegelians. Later refinements of the theory were a consequence of theoretical and practical battles with the anarchists, especially Proudhon, Bakunin, and their followers. We must now look at the particular formulations of the theory that emerged.

Although Marx's general conception of the structural origins of the independent state never changed after *The German Ideology*, there is one important part of the theory of the transcendence of the state which had to await further historical development: the theory of the transitional regime and its function in the project of transcending the state. Marx insisted that the special structure of the Paris Commune of 1871 is necessary for establishing working class political power and for intiating the development toward communism and stateless society.

With the addition of Marx's theory of the role of the transitional regime we can clearly distinguish three different formulations of the theory of the transcendence of the state. The confusion over Marx's theory stems partly from the fact of these different modes of expressing the theory. I believe that Marx's arguments about the importance of the specific structure of the transitional regime bind together the various formulations of the theory, allowing us to see the theory as a whole. However, it is first of all necessary for us to examine the distinct formulations of the theory before we try to reconcile them with each other.

Marx's first opportunity to distinguish his theory from that of the anarchists came in his famous response to Proudhon's *The Philosophy of Poverty*: Marx's *The Poverty of Philosophy*. Near the end of the book Marx gave a presentation of his idea that is interesting for two reasons. First, he repeated his constant theme: the abolition of the proletariat is necessarily the abolition of all classes. Secondly, Marx inserted a qualifying phrase which became a standard feature in his and Engels' discussions and which some critics have utilized to either make Marx appear more 'reasonable' or, conversely, to question his sincerity in desiring a stateless society.

After attacking the philosophical and economic ideas of the man who had brought the word 'anarchy' into common parlance, Marx presented his own doctrine.

> The condition for the emancipation of the working class is the abolition of every class, just as the condition for the liberation of the third estate of the bourgeois order was the abolition of all estates and orders. The working class in the course of its development will substitute for the old civil society an association which will exclude classes and their antagonism, and there will be no more political power *properly so-called* [my emphasis], since political power is precisely the official expression of antagonism in civil society.[1]

The expression "properly so-called" suggests that some kind of institution similar to the state will continue to exist after the revolution. Marx used the same phrase a little later in *The Manifesto of the Communist Party*:

> When in the course of development, class distinctions have disappeared, and all production has been concentrated in the hands of a vast association of the whole nation, the public power will lose its political character. Political power, properly so-called, is merely the organized power of one class for oppressing another.[2]

Shlomo Avineri has drawn particular attention to this passage, using it to support his contention that the 'transcendence of the state' means essentially a 'universalization' of the state's content: when the state is no longer a 'class instrument', when it has been purified of its biases, the public power is no longer 'political'.The important point is that a 'public power' would still remain.[3]

Marx and Engels resorted to similar qualifying phrases again and again. For example, in *The Civil War in France* Marx said that the police force was "stripped of its political attributes" by the Communal Constitution.[4] In a letter in 1875 Engels used the phrase "the state as such ceases to exist"[5] and in the well-known passage from *Anti-Duehring* he remarked that the taking possession of the means of production by the state is "its last independent act as a state."[6]

Marx frequently used this kind of formulation particularly in his "Conspectus of Bakunin's *Statism and Anarchy*".[7] Contrary to Bakunin's expectations of a new ruling elite, Marx argued that in communist society "there is no state in the present political sense."[8] He went on to say that,

as soon as the functions have ceased to be political ones, there exists
(1) no government function; (2) the distribution of the general functions has become a business matter, that gives no one domination; (3)
election has none of its present political character.[9]

The ambiguity of the phrases "domination" and "political character" no
doubt would do little to allay Bakunin's fears.

These qualifications have been well-utilized in Richard Adamiak's interpretation of Marx's theory of the transcendence of the state. According
to Adamiak, Marx and Engels never really expected the state to disappear;
they merely said that it will 'change its character'.[10] Any argumentation to
the contrary by Marx and Engels was only political propaganda to win support away from the anarchist movement.

Adamiak's position is strengthened by Marx's most obvious attempt to
convert the followers of anarchism. In the heat of the struggle within the International Marx stated:

To all socialists anarchy means simply this: the aim of the proletarian
movement -- that is to say the abolition of social classes --once
achieved, the power of the state ... will vanish, and the functions of
government become purely administrative.[11]

This was echoed by Engels in his very pointed attack on the anarchists, "On
Authority" (1874):

Why do the anti-authoritarians not confine themselves to crying out
against political authority, the state? All socialists are agreed that the
political state, and with it political authority, will disappear as a result
of the coming social revolution, that is, that public functions will lose
their political character and be transformed into the simple administrative functions of watching over the true interests of society.
But the anti-authoritarians demand that the authoritarian political
state be abolished at one stroke, even before the social conditions
which gave birth to it have been destroyed.[12]

On hearing these statements of Marx and Engels many anarchists probably concluded that the 'transcendence of the state' would be, in the words of
Karl Kautsky, merely a "question of terminology".[13] Or, as Adamiak says,
the only thing that will change in future communist society is the word
"state".[14]

Adamiak's argument would be more persuasive if this were the only formulation of the theory of the transcendence of the state. However, there are two others which do not coincide with this 'change of nature' formulation. Adamiak avoids other passages which make his interpretation untenable.

It is clear that Marx and Engels conceived that some kind of 'public power' would remain in communist society, altered such that it would no longer deserve the appellation 'political' or 'state'. The problem is that Marx and Engels never immediately connected the above arguments to a discussion of formal institutional changes. (There is one exception: the 'police' passage quoted above.) Because Marx separated the 'change of nature' formulation from other formulations of the transcendence of the state, i.e. because he did not connect them in any coherent manner nor argue them simultaneously, the change of the state's content is not related (on the surface) to the change of its form. This gives rise to confusion but ultimately it is to say no more than that Marx did not write a work exclusively on the transcendence of the state. However, this is a serious problem because, as pointed out by Istvan Meszaros, unless one connects the transcendence of the state to concrete institutional change the idea of a 'change of nature' remains an assertion.[15] The meaning and adequacy of this first formulation can only be revealed by showing its relation to the others.

The second formulation of the theory of the transcendence of the state is the one which gives it its popular name: the 'withering away' of the state. It is necessary to quote in full Engels' passage from *Anti-Duehring*:

> The first act in which the state really comes forward as the representative of society as a whole -- the taking possession of the means of production in the name of society -- is at the same time its last independent act as a state. The interference of the state power in social relations becomes superfluous in one sphere after another, and then ceases of itself. The government of persons is replaced by the administration of things and the direction of the processes of production. The state is not 'abolished', it *withers away*. [emphasis in original][16]

Engels here related 'withering away' with the first formulation by the qualifying phrase "as a state" and proceeded to assert two steps to the process: first the state takes over the means of production and, therefore, *by that act*, is no longer a 'state' proper; *then* this 'non-state' becomes increasingly 'superfluous'. In this passage the theory is clearly reminiscent of Saint-Simon.

There are many very troubling aspects to this important passage. When the state establishes itself as sole owner, it becomes truly 'representative', but this ignores Marx's criticism in his critique of Hegel of *any* representative relation between society and 'state'. The idea that the state should do anything in "the name of society" rather than 'society' acting for itself is against the major thrust of the theory.[17]

Secondly, Engels reduced the transcendence of the state to state ownership. According to Marx and Engels' broader theory, 'ownership' is merely an expression of social relations. In order to deprive the state of its basis, social relations would have to be changed. There is no mention of changing social relations in this key passage on the 'withering away' of the state.

Finally, like Saint-Simon, Engels did not connect the transcendence of the state and the alteration of its 'nature' with any *political* structural proposals. There is no indication that the political structure must be transformed in order to initiate the process of transcendence. We are to assume that state ownership begins the development of a 'unity of purpose', i.e. of community. The best known passage on the transcendence of the state ignores all the essential questions.

In another place Engels related the first formulation of the theory, the 'change of nature' of the 'state', to a notion of natural (i.e. not consciously mediated) disappearance of functions. He specifically interpreted those passages in *The Poverty of Philosophy* and *The Manifesto* which are a part of the first formulation in terms of the second.[18]

Although the phrase 'withers away' is limited to the one passage in *Anti-Duehring*, the specific characterization of the process that it expresses was given many times. For example, in a letter against Bakunin's conceptions Engels very succinctly stated his interpretation of the theory of the transcendence of the state.

> Bakunin maintains that it is the *state* which has created capital, that the capitalist has his capital *only by grace of the state*. As, therefore, the state is the chief evil, it is above all the state which must be abolished and then capitalism will go to blazes of itself. We, on the contrary, say: abolish capital, the appropriation of all the means of production by a few, and the state will collapse of itself.[19]

122

In another place Engels said simply, "the state will dissolve of itself and disappear."[20]

Because of Engels' frequent recourse to this formulation of 'dissolution *of itself*' or 'withers away', phrases suggesting an automatic disappearance of the state as a consequence of other processes (i.e. implying that 'statelessness' is merely an epiphenomenon or effect of something else), Avineri concludes that Engels' interpretation of the transcendence of the state was different from that of Marx.[21] This forces Avineri to account for two things: why Marx allowed Engels to repeatedly put forth a misleading position on a politically sensitive doctrine, and Marx's own use of very similar phrases to express the theory.

In a review article in 1852 criticizing a book by the Proudhonist E. de Girardin, Marx discussed the various meanings of the phrase "abolition of the state" for the different political and intellectual groups who used it, pointing to its specific meaning for communists.

> The abolition of the state has meaning with the communists only as the necessary consequence of the abolition of classes, with which the need for organized might of one class to keep the others down automatically disappears.[22]

In his "Conspectus of Bakunin's *Statism and Anarchy*" Marx presented an equally striking 'withering away' formulation. There Marx asserted that, after the revolution, the workers' government would necessarily be building on the basis of the old society, therefore, it "still moves within political forms which more or less belong to it" and "employs means for its liberation which after this liberation fall aside."[23] The tenor of this passage is exactly the same as 'withering away': the transcendence of the state does not depend on the conscious creation of a transitional political form which has inscribed in its very structure the possibility of stateless society.

This second formulation of the transcendence of the state, the 'withering away' thesis, is different from the first in that it underscores some kind of (however limited) institutional change: the 'state' is not merely transformed but actually disappears as an institution. However it is similar to the previous formulation in that political change is not mediated by conscious construction of a different form of government. In both formulations the process of the transcendence of the state is an 'automatic' or 'natural' consequence of change in society.

The second formulation is also limiting in another way. As the above quoted passages against Bakunin demonstrates, Engels seems to have argued that in the main 'withering away' is the *opposite* of anarchism. In this passage Engels merely differed with Bakunin on the *basis* of the state, not on its function as an instrument of privilege. They agree on the role of the state but disagree on what is necessary to abolish it.

This standing of anarchism 'on its feet' does not do justice to the complexity of Marx and Engels' theory nor to the insights of the *anarchists* as to the structural changes necessary to ensure a new society. The foundation of the general anarchist belief that little can be accomplished through recourse to existing political forms is lost in the 'withering away' formulation. It is necessary to acknowledge *both* the insights of the anarchists *and* the social bases of the state's existence, which, as Marx and Engels showed well, the anarchists consistently underestimated.

The first two formulations of the transcendence of the state are severely limited by their failure to consider the real efficacy of political transitional forms for determining the future possibilities of stateless society. If these were the only two formulations we would have reason to agree with those critics who argue that Marx and Engels did not fully appreciate the difficulties that arise from using a state to pass to stateless society.

However there is a third formulation which is in many respects very different from the previous formulations. In this final conception the transcendence of the state is expressed (1) as the "absorption" of state functions by society, not their absolute disappearance, and (2) the absorption of the state is a process *necessarily* and *consciously* initiated by the "smashing" of the existing state apparatus, not a mere consequence of vague 'social' development. This raises the conscious construction of an essentially different kind of 'state' to a central role in progress toward stateless society. This also amounts to recognition of the argument of the anarchists that the existing state is incapable of bringing about a new society and acknowledgement that the future society must be contained in some manner in the forms of the transition. Furthermore, this last formulation can be interpreted such that it includes the other two formulations and lays the foundation for presenting the theory as a coherent whole.

The idea of an "absorption" of state functions by society has been seen in various arguments of Marx in the early works. It is the basis of Marx's critique of Hegel's political philosophy, underlying the expression of the transcendence of the state he gave there and his peculiar use of the term "democracy".[24] A few months after the *Critique*, in "On the Jewish Question," Marx explicitly formulated the transcendence of the state as the "resumption" of "citizenship".[25]

The major expression of this idea, however, is Marx's commentary on the anarchist-dominated Paris Commune of 1871, *The Civil War in France*. In this work Marx clearly conceived the transcendence of the state *not* as a future development but as a crucial aspect of the revolutionary *transition* to communism. The transcendence of the state is not simply the completion of a long historical trek to 'full communism' but is a part of the revolutionary struggle for and defense of communism itself. The political form of the transitional state is very important for progress toward stateless society.

According to Marx, the Commune was far from being a 'state'; on the contrary, it

> was a revolution against the *state* itself, this supernaturalist abortion of society, a resumption by the people for the people of its own social life.[26]

The previous French state, which was not an exception but the "classical development",[27] was a "parasite".

> Every solitary interest engendered by the relations of social groups was separated from society itself, fixed and made independent of it and opposed to it in the form of state interest ...[28]

In so doing the state was reinforced in its position as a structure independent of civil society, "pretending to be its ideal counterpart."[29]

Although the Commune did not have time to complete its development, the independent state institution was to be completely "smashed" by the Commune.

> The unity of the nation was not to be broken, but, on the contrary, to be organized by the Communal Constitution and to become a reality by the destruction of the state power which claimed to be the embodiment of that unity independent of, and superior to, the nation itself. While the merely repressive organs of the old government were to be amputated, its legitimate functions were to be wrested from an authority usurping pre-eminence over society itself ...[30]

In this way the Commune "breaks the modern state power."[31]

We must be very careful in identifying precisely what Marx said here. The idea that only the "purely repressive" functions of the state will be abolished while certain "legitimate functions" of the state remain suggests that a 'state' will remain to perform these functions. This is the way Hal Draper appears to interpret this passage.[32]

However Marx actually states that the "legitimate functions" which will persist will be exercised by "society itself". The remaining functions are not retained as a basis for the continuance of the 'state' but are, in some manner, "absorbed" by society. Even though certain functions remain, they are not to be embodied in a 'state'.

The Commune 'absorbed' these functions in that it was structured as a completely responsive and responsible government. The measures and constitution of the Commune are well-known: the replacement of a standing army by a citizens' militia; the election of delegates to positions always subject to immediate recall; all governmental jobs to be performed at worker's wages; the binding of delegates by "formal instructions" (the "mandat imperatif"); the unification of legislative and executive functions; the reduction of the tasks of the central Commune; and the destruction of the "sham independence" of the judiciary and the police.[33]

Particularly important here is the destruction of an autonomous force for repression and its replacement by a militia. In several places Engels noted (as did Lenin after him) that the creation of an armed force separate from society is the major institution of the state.[34] Consequently the first order of the day was to abolish "the institution of a *public force* which is no longer immediately identical with the people's organization of themselves as an armed power."[35] Marx reported that:

> The first decree of the Commune, therefore, was the suppression of the standing army, and the substitution for it of the armed people.[36]

This was particularly apropos in France because the National Guard, the citizens' militia in Paris, had led the resistance and was the main structure of the Commune.

Secondly, Engels pointed to two of these procedures as "infallible means" to prevent the "transformation of the state and the organs of the state from servants of society into masters of society": universal suffrage with immediate recall and worker's wages for all government positions.[37] One index of the importance of these measures is that both were quickly jettisoned by socialist governments.

The measures of the Commune were a combination of turning certain functions over to society as a whole (especially the means of coercion; "the people do their police business themselves") and making other functions responsible to the people. In this way the Commune amounted to a complete repudiation of 'representative' government in any meaningful sense of the term. The Communal Constitution

> restored to the social body all the forces hitherto absorbed by the state parasite feeding upon, and clogging the free movement of society.[38]

For this reason Marx called the Commune "the direct antithesis to the Empire",[39] its "definite negation".[40]

In other places there are variants of the theme of the 'absorption' of state functions. In the *Critique of the Gotha Programme* Marx referred to "converting the state from an organ superimposed on society into one thoroughly subordinate to it," a similar idea although not well articulated.[41] It is clear that Marx was fully aware of the drastic structural changes necessary to institute this radical democracy. Furthermore, the Commune is compatible with Marx's earlier argument that the realization of democracy is actually its abolition as a separate stsate form.

Marx's description of the Commune as a 'democracy' has caused much confusion. For example, Maximilien Rubel believes that Marx was "a revolutionary communist only in theory, while he was a bourgeois democrat in practice."[42] There was nothing remotely "bourgeois" about Marx's endorsement of the structure of the Commune. As early as his *Critique of Hegel* and "On the Jewish Question" Marx had quite clearly seen the distinction between 'bourgeois democracy' and real democracy, labelling the former a "republic". Rubel himself notes the relation of Marx's early conception of democracy and his later conception of communism.[43] What Rubel fails to see is that "democracy ... maintained and raised to a higher significance"[44] is dependent upon the structural changes of the Commune. It does not proceed directly from 'bourgeois democracy'.

Marx's characterization of and support for the Commune makes clear the complete inadequacy of Engels' formulation of the transcendence of the state in *Anti-Duehring*, of the state becoming "truly representative" and taking possession of the means of production "in the name of society". In one place in his drafts to *The Civil War in France* Marx explicitly rejected this conception.

> That the revolution is made *in the name* of and confessedly *for* the popular masses, i.e. the producing masses, is a feature that this revolution has in common with all its predecessors. The new feature is that the people, after the first use, have not disarmed themselves and surrendered their power into the hands of republican mountebanks of the ruling classes, that by the constitution of the Commune, they have taken the actual management of their revolution into their own hands and found at the same time, in case of success, the means to hold it in the hands of the people itself, displacing the state machinery, the government machinery of the ruling classes by a government machinery of their own.[45]

In a letter Engels himself recognized that mere legislation 'by the people' is not revolutionary; on the other hand, "*administration* by the people, that would be something."[46]

All of the above comments by Marx on the role of the Commune in the transcendence of the state must be taken in conjunction with other considerations. The most important is that, although the Communal structure is necessary for the development of communism, the 'Commune' and 'communism' are not identical. Ultimately the Commune is a *means* for social change, not an end-in-itself. By its particular structure the Commune initiated the development toward communism:

> The political rule of the producer cannot coexist with the perpetuation of his social slavery. The Commune was therefore to serve as a lever for uprooting the economical foundations upon which rests the existence of classes, and therefore class rule.[47]

However, the Commune was no more than "the political form at last discovered under which to work out the economical emancipation of labor."[48] The mistake of anarchist interpretations was to take the political form as the final end rather than a step in the process of development.[49]

The complete transcendence of the state depends upon the abolition of classes and, although the Commune was essential to this goal, it is distinguishable from it. The Commune would have to live through class struggles (with the peasantry as well as the bourgeoisie), but these struggles would take place in a "more rational and humane way" because of its existence.[50] Since the Commune was only an initial step on a long road, Marx said of its measures, "there is nothing socialist in them but their tendency."[51] He repeated this in a letter on the tenth anniversary of the Commune, adding that the Commune could not have been socialist because of the underdevelopment of French conditions at the time.[52]

Nevertheless, even though the Commune was not specifically socialist nor was that the intention of many of its actors, the conclusion of Marx's *The Civil War in France* is that of the absolute necessity of the creation of a new kind of power to initiate the development of communism. Marx very clearly stated the primary point:

> The working class cannot simply lay hold of the ready-made state machinery and wield it for their [*sic*] own purposes. The political instrument of their enslavement cannot serve as the political instrument of their emancipation.[53]

Somewhat later Engels asserted that this new political form "must necessarily in the end have led to communism."[54]

Marx's conception of the Commune and the transitional regime in general is that of "the reabsorption of the state power by society as its own living forces." The political form necessary for the transition to communism is no longer a 'state'; it is not force which stands in an independent relation to society. In a famous letter Engels suggested that for this reason the word 'state' should be dropped from discussions of the transitional regime and the German word "Gemeinwesen" be adopted as the equivalent to the French "Commune".[55] It is interesting to note that the word "Gemeinwesen" is the same word Marx sometimes used in his early works to characterize the "true state".[56]

Marx's discussion of the Commune is not entirely compatible with his other writings on the state and for that reason his sincerity has been questioned. First, Marx's support for the Commune makes political *form* very important, which is different from his usual conception of the role of the political. Secondly, the Commune was dominated by Proudhonists and Blanquists, Marx's political antagonists, whose future actions and program were difficult to predict. It is not likely that the Commune's leaders would have pushed the Commune in the direction Marx thought appropriate. Thirdly, Marx and Engels were opposed to the idea of a workers' uprising in France only a few months before the Commune, condemning such an uprising as "premature".[57]

Many have cast doubt on Marx's support for the Commune. The mass of evidence, however, indicates that Marx was capable of learning from history (unlike many of his disciples) and that he regarded the Commune, no matter how ill-timed or badly led, as an essentially progressive step for the proletariat. It is absolutely clear that, even if one rejects the *specific* form of the French Commune of 1871, a drastic restructuring of political power is necessary to begin the process of the transcendence of the state.

The arguments about Marx's 'true' feelings about the Commune are actually a consequence of the deeply ambiguous nature of the Commune itself. Marx once referred to it as "that sphinx so tantalizing to the bourgeois mind,"[58] perfectly capturing the multiplicity of interpretations to which it was open.

The ambiguity of the Commune, of its class composition and likely future course, is founded in its character as an "expansive political form."[59] By this Marx meant two things: first, its political structure was such that it could be adopted on several different levels, from local government to the highest national level. Secondly, it was 'expansive' in that it opened new possibilities for political participation of the vast majority of the population, regardless of class position. Like the bourgeois revolutions, this revolution really contained the interests of the majority of groups of the populace. It was open to various interpretations because it realized the interests of many different social groups, not just the proletariat. Most importantly, it was in the interests of the peasantry and the petty bourgeoisie. Marx clearly saw this (and, as usual, was comparing this revolution's possibilities for claiming 'universality' with the previous bourgeois revolutions) when he headed one of the chapters of his draft to *The Civil War in France*: "The Communal Revolution as the Representative of All Classes of Society Not Living upon Foreign Labor."[60] The Paris Commune was open to a variety of interpretations because it comprised the interests of several social groups, each of which supported it for its own reasons. Nonetheless, all of these groups recognized that the revolution was under the hegemony of the proletariat.

Marx and Engels' discussion of the Commune has two consequences for the theory of the transcendence of the state. First, it elevates to extreme importance the structure of the transitional regime; political revolution is necessary for initiating the process. Far from an automatic development

caused by social or economic change (e.g. an increase in the productive forces), the transcendence of the state begins with conscious political construction.

Secondly, their analysis is immediately related to Marx's early works
on the transcendence of the state in that the emphasis is on the 'absorption'
of state functions, not their absolute abolition. This brings out very well the
real difference between Marx's theory of stateless society and the demands
of the anarchists. The theoretical dispute with the anarchists does not merely concern the social bases of the state nor the tempo of the transition to
stateless society ('abolition' versus 'withering away'; 'act' or 'process'),
although it certainly does include these. The essential distinction of the
'transcendence of the state' from anarchist theory is that many of the functions *do not disappear*: they are "absorbed". As Marx insisted in his critique of Hegel, an apparatus remains; it 'merely' loses its privileged position
relative to society and becomes completely the servant of society. The crucial problem of course is analyzing the possibilities and conditions for the
establishment of such a regime.

There are several difficulties with Marx's analysis of the Paris Commune which have been very important for later socialist development. First,
one of the key issues for later socialist regimes and socialist theory is the
problem of centralization versus decentralization. Marx was very ambiguous on the precise status of centralized functions in the Paris Commune.

> What Paris wants is to break up that factitious unitarian system, so
> far as it is the antagonist of the real living union of France and a mere
> means of class rule.[61]

There can be no question that some centralized functions would remain;
Marx had no intention of completely destroying centralization, the "powerful coefficient of social production."[62] However, the manner in which this
centralization was to be reconciled with vigorous democracy 'from below'
was not sufficiently explained by Marx and persists as a major dilemma of
existing socialism.

A second problem, related to the centralization question, is the precise
way in which the means of production will come under collective control.
Engels suggested much later that direct workers' control of factories was
the primary method of the Commune.

> [B]y far the most important decree of the Commune instituted an organization of large-scale industry and even of manufacture which was not only to be based on the association of workers in each factory, but also to combine all these associations in one great union ...[63]

If indeed this was its most important decree one would expect Marx to give it some attention. Although Marx did mention that the Commune turned factories over to workers' associations ("'possible' communism"),[64] it must be remembered that this only applied to factories that had been closed, either as a protest by their owners or simply abandoned in the revolution.[65] If there was a general plan for creating a network of worker-controlled factories, Marx did not discuss it. The whole issue was not as clearly explained by Marx as Engels reported later.

This, however, is a crucial question for existing socialist theory and practice: who controls the means of production, associations of workers or the quasi-state? Since Marx assumed that the Communal structure would survive and ensure worker control of government, the issue did not have the same urgency as at present. However, direct worker control of the workplace was to become the most promising means for the articulation of power on different levels, producing, to some degree, real worker control. Marx and Engels' most frequent statements, on the other hand, suggest 'nationalization', not what is now called 'real socialization', of the means of production.

A third difficulty with Marx's account of the Paris Commune is the future of the Commune. Commentators disagree over whether Marx implied that the Communal structure itself would 'wither away'. In *State and Revolution* Lenin asserted that the Commune, i.e. even the most well-developed democracy, will eventually disappear because it is also a state form. However, if the Commune was as successful at 'absorbing' state functions as Marx claimed, there would be no reason for it to disappear. Unfortunately, although Marx insisted that the Commune would undergo 'changes', neither Marx nor Engels elaborated on the ultimate fate of the Commune and therefore in their work the question is unresolved.

Finally, there is a major assumption of Marx and Engels in all of their discussions of the transitional regime: like their predecessor Saint-Simon, they expected a unity of purpose to be largely a natural consequence of the revolution. As in his critique of Hegel, Marx assumed that the development of community would be rather easily accomplished once the exploiting classes were overthrown. The establishment of a substantial consensus on all major questions the new society would face is imperative for the success of the democratic structure of the Commune. This optimism regarding the overcoming of the disruptive forces which Marx had identified in previous works is one of the recurring features of Marx's theory.

At no time did Marx give a detailed, rigorous analysis of the forces of the division of labor and classes in conjunction with arguments of exactly how the transitional regime will dismantle these structures. The problem with his theory is that parts of his argument are in some works and parts are in others. Even his discussion of the Paris Commune is more suggestive than a precise answer to qusetions that were to be of great importance to post-revolutionary societies. If the theory of the transcendence of the state is to lose its utopian appearance, we must delineate at least some of the structural changes of society and government that will produce it. We cannot assert, as so many are content to do, that, once we achieve 'classlessness', the exercise of power or the goals of the productive process will be unproblematic (especially if we don't better define 'classless'). The structure which establishes this order must be argued; we must go beyond Saint-Simon.

For all of its problems, Marx's discussion of the Paris Commune does present a distinct third formulation of the theory of the transcendence of the state. In the next chapter it is possible to indicate the main features of the theory and show how the three different formulations can be comprehended as a coherent whole.

1. Marx, *The Poverty of Philosophy* (New York: International Publishers, 1973), p. 174.

2. Marx and Engels, "The Manifesto of the Communist Party," in *The Revolutions of 1848: Political Writings Volume I*, edited and introduced by Davuid Fernbach (New York: Random House, 1974), p. 87.

3. Shlomo Avineri, *The Social and Political Thought of Karl Marx* (London: Cambridge University Press, 1968), p. 207.

4. Marx, "The Civil War in France," in *The First International and After: Political Writings Volume III*, edited and introduced by David Fernbach (New York: Random House, 1974), p. 209.

5. Engels, letter to Bebel (March 18-28, 1875), in *Marx-Engels Selected Correspondence* (Moscow: Progress Publishers, 1975), pp. 275-276.

6. Engels, *Herr Eugen Duehring's Revolution in Science [Anti- Duehring]* (New York: International Publishers, 1976), p. 307.

7. See Bakunin's original work, "Statism and Anarchy", in *Bakunin on Anarchy*, edited and introduced by Sam Dolgoff (New York: Alfred A. Knopf, 1972).

8. Marx, "Conspectus of Bakunin's *Statism and Anarchy*," in *The First International and After*, p. 336.

9. Ibid., p. 336.

10. Richard Adamiak, "The 'Withering Away of the State': A Reconsideration," *The Journal of Politics* Volume 32, Number 1 (February 1970).

11. Marx, "The Alleged Splits in the International," in *The First International and After*, p. 314.

12. Engels, "On Authority," in *The Marx-Engels Reader*, edited by Robert Tucker (New York: W.W. Norton and Co., Inc., 1978), pp. 732-733.

13. Karl Kautsky, *The Labor Revolution* (London: George Allan and Unwin, Ltd., 1925), p. 58.

14. Adamiak, op. cit., p. 9.

15. Istvan Meszaros, "Political Power and Dissent in Post-Revolutionary Societies," *New Left Review* Number 108 (March-April 1978), p. 4.

16. Engels, *Anti-Duehring*, p. 307.

17. See Marx's critique of representation in Chapter Two, supra. See also Rudolf Bahro, *The Alternative in Eastern Europe* (London: New Left Books/Verso, 1978), p. 31.

18. Engels, letter to van Patten (April 18, 1883), in *Marx-Engels Selected Correspondence*, p. 341.

19. Engels, letter to Theodor Cuno (January 24, 1872), in ibid., p. 257.

20. Engels, letter to Bebel (March 18-28, 1875), in ibid., p. 275.

21. Avineri, *The Social and Political Thought of Karl Marx*, pp. 202-203.

22. Marx, "Review of E. de Girardin, *Le Socialisme et l' impot*," in *Marx-Engels Collected Works* Volume 10 (New York: International Publishers, 1978), pp. 333-334. This passage was quoted at length by Engels in an article on anarchism (October 1850), ibid., p. 486.

23. Marx, "Conspectus of Bakunin's *Statism and Anarchy*," p. 338.

24. See Chapter Two, supra.

25. Marx, "On the Jewish Question," in *Karl Marx: Early Writings*, introduced by Lucio Colletti (New York: Vintage Books, 1975), p. 234.

26. Marx, "The First Draft of 'The Civil War in France'," in *The First International and After*, p. 249.

27. Marx, "The Civil War in France," p. 211.

28. Marx, "First Draft," p. 247.

29. Ibid., p. 247.

30. Marx, "The Civil War in France," p. 210.

31. Ibid., p. 211.

32. Hal Draper, "The Death of the State in Marx and Engels," *The Socialist Register 1970*, edited by Ralph Miliband and John Saville (London: Merlin Press, 1970), p. 295.

33. Marx, "The Civil War in France," p. 210.

34. Engels, *The Origin of the Family, Private Property, and the State* (New York: International Publishers, 1973), p. 180 and pp. 229-230.

35. Ibid., pp 229-230.

36. Marx, "The Civil War in France," p. 209.

37. Engels, "Introduction of 1891 to *The Civil War in France*," in *Writings on the Paris Commune (Marx and Engels)*, edited and introduced by Hal Draper (New York: Monthly Review Press, 1971), p. 33.

38. Marx, "The Civil War in France," p. 211.

39. Ibid., p. 208.

40. Marx, "First Draft," p. 249.

41. Marx, "Critique of the Gotha Programme," in *The First International and After*, p. 354.

42. Maximilien Rubel, "Notes on Marx's Conception of Democracy," *New Politics*, Winter 1962, p. 79.

43. Ibid., p. 89.

44.Ibid., p. 89.

45. Marx, "First Draft," p. 261.

46. Engels, letter to Bebel (March 18-28, 1875), p. 275.

47. Marx, "The Civil War in France," p. 212.

48. Ibid., p. 212.

49. Marx, "The Alleged Splits in the International," pp. 307-308.

50. Marx, "First Draft," p. 253. In this place Marx also called the Commune a "rational medium". See also Marx, "The Civil War in France," p. 213.

51. Marx, "First Draft," p. 262.

52. Marx, letter to Ferdinand Domela Nieuwenhuis (February 12, 1881), in *Marx- Engels Selected Correspondence*, p. 318.

53. This full quote is from the "Second Draft of 'The Civil War in France'," in *Writings on the Paris Commune (Marx-Engels)*, edited by Draper, p. 196. The second sentence was dropped for stylistic reasons in the final version: "The Civil War in France," in *The First International and After*, p. 206. See also Engels' preface to the 1888 English edition (quoting the 1872 German edition) of "The Manifesto of the Communist Party," in *The Revolutions of 1848*, p. 66.

54. Engels, "Introduction of 1891 to *The Civil War in France*," p. 31 and p. 33. In Draper's version of the first draft Marx is quoted on the Commune as saying, "Whatever therefore its fate in Paris, it will make *le tour du monde*." In Draper, *Writings on the Paris Commune*, p. 151.

55. Engels, letter to Bebel (March 18-28, 1875), p. 275.

56. See Arthur F. McGovern, "The Young Marx on the State," *Science and Society* Volume 34, Number 4, p. 442 (footnote).

57. Engels, letter to Marx (September 12, 1870), in *Marx-Engels Selected Correspondence*, p. 234. See also Adamiak, op. cit., p. 14 and passim; and Karl Korsch, "Revolutionary Commune" [1929], in *Karl Korsch: Revolutionary Theory*, edited and introduced by Douglas Kellner (Austin: University of Texas Press, 1978), p. 209.

58. Marx, "The Civil War in France," p. 206.

59. Ibid., p. 212.

60. Marx, "First Draft," p. 258.

61. Ibid., p. 267.

62. Marx, "The Civil War in France," p. 211.

63. Engels, "Introduction of 1891 to *The Civil War in France*," p. 31.

64. Marx, "The Civil War in France," p. 213.

65. Marx, "First Draft," pp. 236-237.

Chapter 8

The Theory as a Whole

By the 'state' Marx and Engels meant an institution that embodies community. It is autonomous from society because its primary function is to ensure the unity of a fragmented whole. In preserving the capitalist mode of production the state preserves social relations which are exploitative class relations, i.e. it maintains the social position of the bourgeoisie. It is the condition of the rule of the bourgeoisie *as a class* and in order to serve the bourgeoisie as a class it must be free from the domination of the individual bourgeois or substantial fractions of the bourgeoisie. It is not always successful at this but this is its ideal vocation.

According to Marx and Engels the main bases of disunity of society are the existence of classes and the division of labor, which is the specific form of existence of 'classes', properly so-called. The state will be transcended as these bases are eliminated, a process over time implying a transitional period. The idea of a transitional period, between what Marx called the "first" and "higher" phases of communism, was popularized by Lenin as the distinction between "socialism" and "communism".

We must not conceive of these two 'phases' as well-demarcated, mutually exclusive 'stages'. 'Socialism' is the transition to 'communism'; this is its only definition.[1] As such, future forms must be inscribed in the transition itself. The 'transcendence of the state' is not something confined to "several generations hence",[2] although it may only be completed then. The transitional regime must be constructed such that it is already 'not really a state', structurally prefiguring its further transcendence in the future. The contrary interpretation of the process as mutually exclusive 'stages' is one of the ideological means by which existing socialist societies justify the wide range of centralized state activities. The transcendence of the state is considered an essentially different process from existing state forms and procedures.

Marx and Engels gave varying formulations of the transcendence of the state in order to indicate its different features. The primary formulation, the one which informs the others, is the 'absorption' of state functions by society. This 'absorption' is initiated by the assumption of power by the working class through the establishment of a radically democratic regime

140

and progress toward collective ownership of the means of production. A regime such as the Paris Commune of 1871 allows the immediate participation of the vast majority of the population. Since the majority rules, there is no need for an institution standing apart from and superior to society; only minority regimes require an embodiment of unity and the representation of the 'general will'. As Marx said against Bakunin, "with collective ownership the so-called people's will vanishes, to make way for the real will of the cooperative."[3] With the establishment of immediate political expression of the community, the "illusory community" or "previous substitutes for community" become unnecessary.[4] On this point it is very easy to see the relation between Marx's early critique of Hegel and all of his later formulations.

One key function of the state that is absorbed is the exercise of coercion. The means of violence is wielded by society as a whole, on a reduced scale of course because a large force is not necessary to keep down a minority. The function of coercion continues to 'wither away' as the expropriated become reconciled to the new society and "sporadic slave-holders insurrections" subside.[5] Furthermore, the intellectual leadership of the working class (the "natural trustees" of the interests of the peasants) is reduced as a centralized function when the bases of small plot production and the isolating cultural conditions of the rural producers are abolished.[6]

The transitional period is not an easy one, neither in practice nor in theory. Recognition of the persistence of classes and class struggle throughout the transitional period, i.e. the recognition of a 'transitional period' itself, is one of the things that separates Marx's theory from anarchism. In response to Bakunin's fears of this transitional governmental form, Marx insisted that:

> as long as the other classes, especially the capitalist class, still exists [sic], so long as the proletariat still struggles with it [sic] (for when it attains governmental power its enemies and the old organization of society have not yet vanished), it must employ *forcible* means, hence governmental means. It is itself still a class and the economic conditions from which the class struggle and the existence of classes derive have still not yet disappeared and must forcibly be either removed out of the way or transformed, this transformation process being forcibly hastened.[7]

In the transitional period the proletariat is still in the process of overthrowing the "old form of society" and therefore requires a strong government. Nonetheless it is important to remember that this 'government' is not a 'state'. It retains aspects of a state insofar as it must maintain a high degree of centralization in order to best employ "forcible means" in the class struggle. It is not a state in that it maintains the radical democratic form of the Commune which allows society to have complete control over, i.e. 'absorb', governmental functions.

All of Marx's comments on the transitional period are necessarily difficult because the transitional regime proceeds in the midst of class struggle. For this reason the goals of the transitional regime are contradictory: to ensure the political supremacy of one class and to simultaneously create a truly democratic regime. The essential tension between radical democracy and the supremacy of the proletariat is demonstrated in the most ambiguous phrase in all of Marx's work: the "dictatorship of the proletariat". This phrase is only made more difficult by Engels' well-known remark:

> Of late, the Social-Democratic philistine has once more been filled
> with wholesome terror at the words: Dictatorship of the Proletariat.
> Well and good, gentlemen, do you want to know what this dictator-
> ship looks like? Look at the Paris Commune. That was the Dictator-
> ship of the Proletariat.[8]

In what sense the radically democratic Commune was a "dictatorship" remains unclear, to the detriment of socialist political theory.

Marx himself once said that the transitional measures of the *Manifesto* were and *had* to be contradictory.[9] Marx and Engels did not ignore the tensions of the transition but neither did they sufficiently explore them. Unfortunately neither can they be explored here. For the purposes of this work we have to simply accept the contradictions of the transitional period, the establishment of direct democracy and the supremacy of the proletariat, as an example of what Lenin called the "dialectics of living history."[10]

Besides the 'class power' function which necessitates the existence of a transitional 'state-form', there is also an 'economic development' function which marks the transition *as* a 'transition'. The complete transformation of society requires an increase in the forces of production. Full communism cannot be achieved until "all the springs of cooperative wealth flow more abundantly."[11] We can infer that what Marx said of the capitalist state in this regard is also true of the socialist transitional regime; it is necessary to employ

> the power of the state, the concentrated and organized force of society, to hasten, hothouse fashion, the process of transformation ... and to shorten the transition.[12]

As with the class struggle, this function also will gradually 'wither away' with a higher level of production.

In the various struggles of the transitional period it is the existence of radical democracy that justifies Marx and Engels' portrayal of the transitional regime as 'not really a state'. It is only this which keeps a new embodiment of community, separate from and superior to society, from developing and also guarantees further progress toward complete 'stateless' society. The maintenance of this democracy is, therefore, of utmost importance.

The 'withering away' formulation refers (1) to the gradual reduction of functions that have already been 'absorbed' by society and (2) to the decentralization of power which is a consequence of the transformation of existing social conditions. As the class struggle subsides and progress is made toward 'abundance', a 'unity of purpose' is easier to establish. However, it is extremely important to remember that the functions that were formerly exercised by a 'state' and in the transitional period are performed by the Communal government *do not* completely disappear. In the *Critique of the Gotha Programme* Marx asked (but did not answer) the question: "what social functions will remain that are analogous to the present functions of the state?"[13] Although it is difficult to establish from the texts, it appears that Marx and Engels expected a function of coordination to persist into the future, even *after* the transitional period: even an orchestra needs an orchestra leader.[14]

It is precisely the existence of 'analogous functions' even in fully developed communism which necessitated the third formulation of the theory of the transcendence of the state: that the 'state' will lose its 'political character'. Throughout his work Marx argued that the chief function of the state is to create unity. It is this function which requires an independent embodiment of unity and community. The state is in its very essence not responsible to society because 'society' has no homogeneity to counterpose to the unity of the state. This function of unity and the corresponding relation of independence of the state to society is what Marx and Engels referred to as its 'political character'. The governing apparatus loses this aspect when (1) there is no longer any reason for an independent embodiment of unity and community, and (2) when it is no longer used in the interests of a minority. A governing apparatus remains but does not stand in a privileged relation to other social functions. It becomes, as Marx -- following Saint-Simon --always expressed it, 'just another branch of the division of labor'. The 'political character' of the state is merely another way of expressing its independence and its class bias. Avineri and others err in only regarding the class bias as the basis of its 'political character'. Unless we keep in mind both aspects the theory becomes a variant of liberalism, merely concerned with the purification of the 'public power'.

The governing apparatus loses its political character over time. It is a process that takes place with the success of the radically democratic transitional regime and the elimination of classes. The abolition of classes removes *both* of the reasons for the existence of an institution embodying unity. It simultaneously eliminates interclass and intraclass fragmentation and class bias.

The change in nature of the governing apparatus has also been argued by Saint-Simon, Engels, and various commentators on the theory as a change in the nature of 'authority'. Contrary to the anarchists, authority does not disappear; as Engels insisted in the article "On Authority", authority is necessary to any interdependent productive enterprise.[15] However, with the development of a unity of purpose, authority stands in a different relation to members of society because there is a greater identification with all authority as the 'will of the cooperative'. Nonetheless, as with all of the above arguments, the important issue is not this greater identification but the structure which realizes it, i.e. the transitional regime. It is always the specific structure of the transitional regime and the efficacy of its policies which determine the reasonableness of the theory of the transcendence of the state.

There is a formal change which Marx and Engels mentioned in various places (especially in *The German Ideology*) that is intimately related to the alteration of the nature of authority: the change in the nature of authority manifests itself as the disappearance of law.

> As far as law is concerned, we with many others have stressed the
> opposition of communism to law, both political and private, as also
> in its most general form as the rights of man.[16]

Although Marx and Engels never really explored the issue at length, the 'disappearance of law' must be briefly examined here.

Marx believed that 'law' is a consequence of the necessity of (1) creating a common 'will' for 'classes' (in a precise sense) and (2) for the rule of classes in the guise of the general interest.[17] 'Law', unlike 'privilege', is universal, i.e. it applies to all equally regardless of their social position, and therefore it is intimately related to the institution of the governing apparatus as the separate embodiment of universality. With the dissolution of classes and the rule of the 'general interest', 'law', properly so-called, will no longer be necessary.

Marx did not explain what will replace 'law' but the great majority of commentators have interpreted him to mean that law will be replaced by a less formal exercise of authority, i.e. 'moral persuasion'. For example, Lukacs took this position:

> The ultimate objective of communism is the construction of a society
> in which freedom of morality will take the place of legal compulsion
> in the regulation of all behavior.[18]

This very popular argument is misleading, however, in that it conflates the two issues of 'coercion' and 'legal form'. For example, 'coercion' is exercised in primitive communities without taking a developed legal form. The development of law, like the state, does not rest on the necessity of coercion but on the necessity of a universal, independent structure standing above other social relations and creating unity. 'Law' corresponds to this modern function of unity and Marx distinguished it from 'privilege' for precisely that reason.

Evgeny B. Pashukanis gave a more interesting interpretation of the change of nature of authority and the disappearance of law by contrasting legal regulation with other forms of regulation. Pashukanis believed that the legal form rests on the individualized conflict that is a necessary part of exchange society. All regulation will not disappear in a communist society but it will differ from 'law' in that its function will be purely one of coordination.

As an example Pashukanis pointed to the difference of the coordinating authority of a railroad timetable and that of 'law' proper.[19]

Pashukanis' analysis is persuasive and appears to be in accord with the thrust of Marx's argument. It rests on the fundamental assumption he shared with Marx, Engels, and Saint-Simon: under certain social conditions a substantial unity of purpose can emerge. The advance of Marx and Engels over Saint-Simon is that they clearly indicated the conditions necessary for this unity: radical democracy and the abolition of classes through common ownership.

In explicating their notion of how the state loses its 'political character' Marx and Engels most frequently resorted to Saint-Simon's terms. One example among many is Engels' praise in *Anti-Duehring* for Saint-Simon's insights of 1816:

> And if the recognition that economic conditions are the basis of political institutions here shows itself only in embryo, nevertheless the transformation of political government over men into the administration of things and the direction of productive processes -- i.e. the abolition of the state about which so much noise has been recently made everywhere -- is already clearly stated.[20]

This transformation rests on the success of the measures promoted by Marx and Engels to establish community on the social level, thereby making its independent institution, a state, superfluous. Whether these measures in the specific form that Marx and Engels argued them can produce this community is the central point by which the theory of the transcendence of the state must be evaluated.

The three formulations by Marx and Engels of the theory of the transcendence of the state are not mutually exclusive. Their connections are not simple and easy but the formulations need not be construed in a contradictory manner. The conception of the 'withering away' of the state and the notion of the state 'losing its political character' are both comprised in the formulation of the 'absorption' of state functions by society.

The absorption of state functions is the process which abolishes the conditions which engender a separate institution embodying unity and community. This process has two interdependent aspects: a transformation of the existing political structure and a transformation of the existing social structure. The 'political' aspect is the establishment of a transitional regime

146

which allows the populace to directly exercise certain functions (especially all coercive functions) and makes the agents of remaining functions responsive to the collective by the institution of 'worker's wages', 'formal instructions' to delegates, and immediate recall. The 'social' aspect is the abolition of classes and the division of labor. With the success of these transformations the very distinction between the 'political' and the 'social' disappears.

In broad terms the movement toward communism is the overcoming of the separation of state and economy engendered by capitalism. In other words, the autonomy of the productive process, the 'economy', is destroyed by subjecting it to popular control and ordering. Production is once again mediated by the community rather than by the market.

In Marx and Engels' conception the abolition of this separation takes the form of the destruction of private property by 'state' ownership of the means of production, i.e. ownership by the transitional government. As previously cited, Engels stated this unequivocally:

> The first act by which the state really comes forward as the representative of society as a whole -- the taking possession of the means of production in the name of society ...[21]

There are stray comments of Marx and Engels which suggest alternatives to 'state' ownership, i.e. cooperative factories, but they are rare and are not integrated into any of the passages on the transcendence of the state.[22] In all of the key passages Marx and Engels depend upon the transitional government as the new owner.

With the abolition of private property, labor-power as a commodity is also abolished. Furthermore, when the exchange of labor is mediated by the 'state', not the market, the law of value no longer functions. This is a very controversial topic but it must be briefly reviewed here.[23]

Under capitalism the exchange of commodities is regulated by the law of value. The value of a particular commodity is determined by the "socially necessary labor-time" it embodies, i.e. the *average* time in a society it takes to produce the thing. The actual labor embodied in any particular commodity is of no consequence for exchange; only the average labor-time necessary to produce the commodity determines its value. The producer receives for his or her product only the value that corresponds to the average time, whether he or she has actually expended more concrete labor or not.

When the *state* regulates the exchange of the product of labor the law of value ceases to function because *concrete* labor is being exchanged, not "socially necessary labor-time". Marx argued in this manner: under capitalism labor is only 'social' by the mediation of the market, i.e. the "estranged community".[24] Under communism, on the other hand, "the social character of production is presupposed;"[25] different labor activities are directly united by the community. The equivalence of labors is not a consequence of the objective processes of the market but of conscious communal control of production. In a communist society,

> it would not be exchange which gave labor its general character, but rather its presupposed communal character would determine the distribution of products. The communal character of production would make the product into a communal, general product from the outset.[26]

Under communism labor is not exchanged through the mediation of things. Different kinds of labor are directly related and considered merely different activities of a social whole. With the exchange of concrete labor, the law of value has no social basis for existence.

This point is extremely important for Marx's conception of communism. Economic laws only result from the *autonomy* of the economic sphere, i.e. they are a consequence of its freedom from direct control. When the actions of people cease to have 'unintended consequences' because of their blind isolation, socio-economic laws cease to exist. This is one of the reasons Marx characterized communism as the 'end to the prehistory of mankind'.

It is fairly common for theorists to speak of the 'laws of a socialist economy' but this is either an inappropriate choice of words or a misunderstanding of (at least) Marx's conception of socialism, broadly defined as the overcoming of the autonomy of the economic. It is also common for Soviet and Eastern European theorists to discover 'laws' of socialist economies but Domenico Mario Nuti has given an interesting interpretation of these 'laws'.

> These pseudo-laws clearly have nothing to do with the Marxian 'laws of motion' of society. They are just part of the official ideology, i.e. are a component of the socialist 'superstructure'.[27]

These 'laws' are discovered in order to legitimize existing policies by giving them an objective-scientific appearance.[28]

It is true that Marx sometimes wrote about 'laws' in a socialist economy[29] but these are not 'laws' in the same sense as capitalism. Marx was using the term 'law' in the same way that Hobbes wrote of "laws of nature": they are merely prudential maxims, guides to rational (goal-satisfying) activities in given circumstances. Their 'compulsive' character depends upon a chosen goal rather than being the result of unconscious interaction.

Abolition of exchange is the major step toward the achievement of collective control of production. As Engels stated succinctly,

> no society can permanently retain the mastery of its own production and the control over the social effects of its process of production unless it abolishes exchange between individuals.[30]

Even under capitalism, as the forces of production grow increasingly complex and interdependent, it is necessary for the state to take direct control of certain key sectors of the economy (especially the infrastructure, i.e. communications and transportation). However there are definite limits to state control under capitalism: it cannot abolish exchange altogether and only this can end the 'anarchy of production'. Nonetheless Marx and Engels did notice these attempts by the capitalist state to curb anarchy, and in the process underlined their own 'statist' orientation: "State ownership of the productive forces is not the solution of the conflict, but it contains within itself the formal means, the key to the solution."[31]

Their insistence on the abolition of exchange and therefore of 'laws' of production clearly reveals Marx and Engels' vision of *communist society as collective control of social interaction.* Contrary to popular belief, Marx and Engels never expressed communist society as some kind of 'harmonious' production attained by the abolition of classes. Communism is collective *control*, not harmony, although a less problematic productive process was expected to be a consequence of collective control.

This must be emphasized because all too often commentators argue that communism is utopian in that it depends on the taming of the 'passions' of people by the removal of class antagonisms. For Marx and Engels, however, communism is a redistribution of power such that collective control can be realized. It is not a subjective-psychological exorcism.

In all the key passages on communist society, *control* (i.e. power) is the concern of Marx and Engels.

Anarchy in social production is replaced by conscious organization
on a planned basis. The struggle for individual existence comes to an
end. And at this point, in a certain sense, man finally cuts himself off
from the animal world, leaves the conditions of animal existence behind him and enters conditions which are really human. The conditions of existence forming man's environment, which up to now have
dominated man, at this point pass under the dominion and control of
man, who now for the first time becomes the real conscious master
of Nature, because and insofar as he has become master of his own
social organization. The laws of his own social activity, which have
hitherto confronted him as external, dominating laws of Nature, will
then be applied by man with complete understanding, and hence will
be dominated by man. ... The objective, external forces which have
hitherto dominated history, will then pass under the control of men
themselves.[32]

The repeated use of the words 'domination', 'mastery', and 'control' leave
no doubt as to Marx and Engels' notion of communism. As Engels summed
it up in a well-known phrase, "It is humanity's leap from the realm of necessity into the realm of freedom."[33]

Equally important for their conception of communism is that this collective control is to be exercised by the "associated laborers" or "associated
producers".[34] According to one report this was somewhat of a "fad" phrase
at the time,[35] but nevertheless it perfectly expresses Marx and Engels'
vision of a free combination of conscious individuals. In *The Origin of the
Family, Private Property, and the State* Engels directly tied this phrase to
the theory of the transcendence of the state.

The society which organizes production anew on the basis of free and
equal association of the producers will put the whole state machinery
where it will then belong -- into the museum of antiquities, next to
the spinning wheel and the bronze axe.[36]

Engels is no doubt correct: collective control of production by associated
producers would make the state machinery superfluous. However, this
proposed association is very much at odds with the 'statist' form in which
the theory is expressed. It is the reef on which communism has foundered
since its inception.

The proposal of government ownership of the means of production creates problems for another crucial aspect of the transcendence of the state: the "abolition of classes". For all of the hints in their work which point in a different direction, Marx and Engels generally reduce the abolition of classes to the abolition of private ownership of the means of production. This is totally inadequate from the standpoint of their own theory because 'ownership' is merely an expression of real material relations of production. The abolition of ownership is distinct from the transformation of the relations of production.

Although we can construct an argument from Marx's work that the abolition of classes must be more than the abolition of private ownership, he did not go beyond governmental ownership in any discussion of the transcendence of the state. This lacuna has been carried over into later discussions of the theory; at no time is the meaning of the 'abolition of classes' explicated. In order to comprehend the importance of the abolition of classes for stateless society we have to go beyond Marx and Engels' analysis in certain respects just as they did that of Saint-Simon.

Marx did mention an aspect of the transcendence of the state which bears on the abolition of classes: the abolition of "class conditions".[37] I take this to mean the abolition of the isolation and powerlessness of individuals which results from the forced division of labor.[38] It is clear that the abolition of the division of labor is necessary to realize a communal order that allows the participation of individuals in control. Unfortunately Marx's arguments are simply too fragmentary to see how the abolition of the division of labor is to be integrated into the theory of the transcendence of the state. It is obvious that it is supposed to be integrated but Marx and Engels never detailed the precise relation.

There is one aspect of the abolition of the division of labor to which Marx and Engels frequently referred: the abolition of the division between 'mental' and 'material' labor. Marx and Engels considered this separation to be the very heart of the division of labor and insisted in *The German Ideology* that the division of labor truly emerges only with this distinction. In a later passage in the *Critique of the Gotha Programme* Marx again placed this in a prominent position:

> In a more advanced phase of communist society, when the enslaving subjugation of individuals to the division of labor, and thereby the

antithesis between intellectual and physical labor have disappeared ...[39]

This is an important statement because it underscores my earlier interpretation of Marx on the meaning of the 'abolition of the division of labor'. The abolition of the mental/material distinction is *not* connected with the abolition of differentiated tasks but with the abolition of "subjugation" to *one* task. The abolition of the mental/material distinction does not mean the abolition of differentiation but the abolition of the separation of the majority from positions of planning and control.

Marx believed that the development of capitalism itself substantially weakens the division of labor in some ways by making most positions more or less 'machine-tending'. He argued that the division of labor tasks peaks in the period of "manufacture" and declines with the later "industrial" phase which depends on the widespread use of machines. However, he further argued that the broader distinction between mental and material labor actually *increases* under industry because the very possibility of using machinery depends on sharply separating 'planning/control' from 'execution'.[40] Again, the only remedy for this is "variation of occupation".

Regardless of its importance for their theory, Marx and Engels only offered us hints as to the relations between classes, class conditions, and the division of labor. Because of the conceptual similarity of these three things, however, we cannot separate their respective 'abolitions'. They can only be formulated separately if we erroneously consider 'classes' to be established by 'ownership' rather than by the actual relations of production. As part of my criticism, I assert the identity of the existence of classes, the existence of the division of labor, and the existence of the state. Although Marx did not explicitly argue so, 'stateless society' and 'classless society' are indeed two sides of the same coin: there can be no 'state' in classless society.

Seen as a whole, Marx's theory of the transcendence of the state has several elements governed by the overriding concern to eliminate the separation of the economic and political spheres by destroying the autonomy of production instituted by private property. The first task is the construction of a completely democratic regime like the Paris Commune, in some manner setting the stage for the abolition of classes and the division of labor. The latter eliminates all of the bases which necessitate an independent embodiment of unity and community.

Unfortunately the theory of the transcendence of the state is inadequate in the form Marx and Engels presented it. Besides the few doubts expressed above, there are internal tensions in Marx's theory that must be addressed. Now that we have seen the theory as a whole, it is to these that we can turn our attention.

1. Etienne Balibar, *On the Dictatorship of the Proletariat* (London: New Left Books, 1977), pp. 62-63.

2. Mentioned by Engels in his "Introduction of 1891 to *The Civil War in France*," in *Writings on the Paris Commune (Marx-Engels)*, edited and introduced by Hal Draper (New York: Monthly Review Press, 1971), p. 34.

3. Marx, "Conspectus of Bakunin's *Statism and Anarchy*," in *The First International and After: Political Writings Volume III*, edited and introduced by David Fernbach (New York: Random House, 1974), p. 336.

4. The latter phrase is in "The German Ideology," *Marx-Engels Collected Works* Volume 5 (New York: International Publishers, 1976), p. 78.

5. Marx, "First Draft of 'The Civil War in France'," in *The First International and After*, p. 253. See also the phrase "slave-holders conspiracy" in Marx, "The Civil War in France," in ibid., p. 221.

6. Marx, "The Civil War in France," p. 211. See also Marx, "First Draft," pp. 256-257.

7. Marx, "Conspectus of Bakunin's *Statism and Anarchy*," p. 333.

8. Engels, "Introduction of 1891 to *The Civil War in France*, p. 34.

9. Marx, letter to Sorge (June 20, 1881), in *Marx-Engels Selected Correspondence* (New York: Progress Publishers, 1975), p. 322.

10. V. I. Lenin, "The State and Revolution," in *Selected works in Three Volumes* Volume 2 (New York: International Publishers, 1967), pp. 326-327.

11. Marx, "Critique of the Gotha Programme," in *The First International and After*, p. 347.

12. Marx, *Capital* Volume 1 (New York: International Publishers, 1974), p. 751.

154

13. Marx, "Critique of the Gotha Programme," p. 355.

14. Marx, *Capital* Volume 3 (New York: International Publishers, 1974), p. 383 and pp. 386-387.

15. Engels, "On Authority," in *The Marx-Engels Reader*, edited by Robert C. Tucker (New York: W.W. Norton and Co., Inc., 1978), pp. 730-733. See also Engels, letter to Theodor Cuno (January 24, 1872), in *Marx-Engels Selected Correspondence*, p. 258.

16. Marx and Engels, "The German Ideology," p. 209.

17. Ibid., p. 92 and passim.

18. Georg Lukacs, "The Role of Morality in Communist Production" [1919], in *Tactics and Ethics: Political Essays 1919-1929* (New York: Harper and Row, Publishers, 1972), p. 48.

19. Evgeny B. Pashukanis, *Law and Marxism: A General Theory* [1924] (London: Ink Links, 1978), p. 81.

20. Engels, *Herr Eugen Duehring's Revolution in Science [Anti-Duehring]* (New York: International Publishers, 1976), p. 283.

21. Ibid., p. 307.

22. Marx, "The Civil War in France," p. 213 (on "possible communism"). See also Marx, "First Draft," pp. 236-237. In the latter Marx noted the Commune's consideration of compensation to owners for seizing workshops that were *already closed*, due to failure or flight by their owners. Also, in his "Introduction of 1891 to *The Civil War in France*," Engels applauded factories run by workers: p. 31. Finally, in *Capital* Volume 3, Marx mentioned "factories owned by the laborers themselves": p. 85.

23. For an alternative view see Stanley Moore, *Marx on the Choice Between Socialism and Communism* (Cambridge: Harvard University Press, 1980), pp. 88-89 and passim. For an excellent account of recent and past argu-

ments on the issue see Alec Nove, *The Economics of Feasible Socialism* (London: George Allan and Unwin, 1983), pp. 20-30.

24. Marx, "Excerpts From James Mill's *Elements of Political Economy*," in *Karl Marx: Early Writings*, introduced by Lucio Colletti (New York: Vintage Books, 1975), pp. 265-266.

25. Marx, *Grundrisse*, translated and introduced by Martin Nicolaus (New York: Vintage Books, 1973), p. 172.

26. Ibid., p. 171.

27. Domenico Mario Nuti, "The Contradictions of Socialist Economies: A Marxian Interpretation," *The Socialist Register 1979*, edited by Ralph Miliband and John Saville (London: Merlin Press, 1979), p. 231.

28. Ibid., pp. 230-231. For Marx's argument on the 'historicity' of the "law of value" see *Capital* Volume 1, p. 536 and the innumerable references in the *Grundrisse*.

29. Marx, *Capital* Volume 3, p. 851, on the future "book-keeping" role of "value". See also *Grundrisse*, pp. 172-173, on the "first economic law": economy of "time".

30. Engels, *The Origin of the Family, Private Property, and the State* (New York: International Publishers, 1973), p. 175.

31. Engels, *Anti-Duehring*, pp. 304-305.

32. Ibid., p. 309-310.

33. Ibid., p. 310.

34. This phrase is quite common: "The German Ideology," p. 80, p. 81, and p. 439; "The Manifesto of the Communist Party," in *The Revolutions of 1848: Political Writings Volume I*, edited and introduced by David Fernbach (New York: Random House, 1974), p. 80 and p. 90; *Anti-Duehring*, p. 305;

156

Capital Volume 3, p. 820. Bertell Ollman once pointed out that even the original German for the phrase in the "Manifesto" -- "vast association of the whole nation" -- reads "assoziierten Individuen".

35. Daniel Tarschys, *Beyond the State: The Future Polity in Classical and Soviet Marxism* (n.p.: Scandinavian University Books, 1971), p. 68.

36. Engels, *The Origin of the Family, Private Property, and the State*, p. 232.

37. Marx, "The Class Struggles in France: 1848-1850," in *Surveys From Exile: Political Writings Volume II*, edited and introduced by David Fernbach (New York: Random House, 1974), p. 123. See also Marx, "Conspectus of Bakunin's *Statism and Anarchy*," p. 333 and p. 337.

38. See Chapter 4, supra.

39. Marx, "Critique of the Gotha Programme," p. 437.

40. Marx, *Capital* Volume 1, p. 361.

Chapter 9

The Political 'Secret' of the Proletariat

One can criticize the theory of the transcendence of the state in a variety of ways. For example, in many places Marx appears to hypostatize 'society', granting it a unity in a post-revolutionary regime that it surely would not achieve easily, if at all. Sometimes he even moves dangerously close to the conception of a 'harmonious' social system. Also, Marx often, against his own principles, seems to suggest that the autonomy of the economy under capitalism is absolute, rather than relative, falling into illusions promoted by non-socialist theorists. There is an underestimation in certain parts of his work of how the capitalist economy is formed as much by the juridical structure establishing specifically *capitalist* property, contracts, liability, etc. as much as by the material requirements of a certain kind of production. In sum, Marx often resorted to modes of expression which fail to live up to his own proposed dialectical relationship between social structure and political structure. One could elaborate these criticisms into a broad critique of Marxian political theory.

In this place it is probably more useful to limit my criticism to two key aspects of Marx's theory of the transcendence of the state: (1) his conception of the proletariat and its significance for political representation, and (2) certain problems for the abolition of the division of labor. I will extend the previous discussion of these two central elements of the theory of the transcendence of the state in this and the succeeding chapter. Hopefully this will allow a more informed evaluation of what is valuable in Marx's theory and what is less reasonable. It will also allow me to consider certain passages in which Marx cast doubts on his own arguments.

The first problem is Marx's conception of the proletariat as essentially a self-constituting political actor. Because of its specific position in the productive process Marx believed that the proletariat escapes the dialectic of representation suffered by other classes, specifically the bourgeoisie and the peasantry. Much of the Marxian tradition has followed this conception of the proletariat as a self-constituting historical subject which 'expresses' itself in politics but does not need political organization (and by extension, a state) in order to act as a class. This notion of the proletariat as basically 'self-emancipating' is the foundation of most Marxian theory of revolution, including *Bolshevik* theory.

One of the manifestations of this conception is that even among those who see a more important role for political organization than Marx did, the relation between 'party' and 'class' is essentially unproblematic. Lukacs went much farther than Marx in recognizing a real need for a political party as "an *autonomous form* of proletarian class consciousness"[1] or "conscious collective will".[2] However, Lukacs, true to Marx's conception, believed that although the party helps organize the proletariat it does not "represent" it in the rigorous sense of autonomously "acting on behalf of" (Lukacs' own distinction).[3]

Lenin argued in a similar manner: the Bolshevik Party is the "disciplined and class-conscious vanguard of the proletariat."[4] Although Lukacs and Lenin both rejected the 'mechanicism' of Marx that the proletariat will of its own slowly achieve consciousness, they still assumed that the party was a 'natural' expression of the proletariat. The party is *part* of the class, its 'pure' expression.[5] Even more sophisticated versions of this notion of the proletariat, such as that of Erik Olin Wright, assert the 'phenomenal' relation of politics to classes. Finally, the Eurocommunist movement, by focusing on the 'hegemony' of the working class in *society*, also denies the independent efficacy of political structures for forming the proletariat into a 'subject', or in *disorganizing* the proletariat.[6]

The major problem for those who conceptualize the proletariat in this manner, as an historical subject constituted solely on the level of the relations of production and therefore having a merely 'expressive' relation to political forms, is to explain why the proletariat does not take advantage of parliamentary opportunities to produce socialist policies.[7] The answer is always a variation on the theme of 'false consciousness': "indoctrination of mass media", "fetishism", or even "embourgeoisification" (Marcuse's *One-Dimensional Man* being the most interesting discussion of the latter).[8] That is, the explanation is sought in every sphere except the political because the political is assumed to be nothing but an *expression* of the class, i.e. it has no independent effect in forging the proletariat into an historical subject.

Perry Anderson has forcibly argued that this explanation of 'false consciousness' is classical 'reformism' in that it makes the issue into one of purely subjective determinations, rather than posing the problem of political structures and the political needs of the proletariat. In so doing it undercuts the argument for "smashing" the state, reducing it to a mere tactic rather than an essential *strategic* move.[9] If we focus simply on subjective phenomena and do not consider how practice and *changing* practice is necessary to alter how people experience the world, i.e. if we do not analyze how political structures are related to class organization and disorganization, then we remain in the abyss of subjectivism.

The consequence of the traditional conception of the proletariat as an historical actor constituted solely by its position in the productive process, achieving consciousness and revolutionary organization more or less "spontaneously" and therefore not needing nor creating independent political forms, is a general underestimation in Marxian theory of political organization and political structures. From the standpoint of this conception we cannot comprehend the difficulties for the revolutionary organization of the proletariat, the problems of existing socialist regimes and why they have developed in the way they have, nor the real prospects for the transcendence of the state.

There are passages in which Marx went somewhat beyond his usual conception of the proletariat as a self-constituting historical subject. At times he did not consider the proletariat capable of acting as a class simply because of its position in the productive process. Rather the proletariat must "organize itself as a class"[10] or be organized "to act as a class".[11]

Marx's discussion of this issue is similar to his portrayal of the problems involved in organizing the bourgeoisie or the peasantry. There are objective divisions within the proletariat which necessitate independent political organization in order for the proletariat to act on its class interests. As with the bourgeoisie, Marx singled out the divisions caused by intra-class competition, asserting it in more severe terms than he did in other places and suggesting that the proletariat is not really a class unless it finds the means to overcome them.

> The separate individuals form a class only insofar as they have to carry on a common battle against another class; in other respects they are on hostile terms with each other as competitors.[12]

We should recall that one of the reasons Marx argued that the peasantry is 'not really' a class is that they cannot enter into struggle with other classes in any direct fashion. Here Marx applied the same criterion to the proletariat, although its prospects are much better.

Marx was keenly aware of how intra-class competition plagued attempts to organize the proletariat into a political party.[13] In *The German Ideology* he even stated that this necessitated political action:

> for proletarians -- owing to the frequent opposition of interests among them arising out of the division of labor -- no other "agreement" is possible than a political one directed against the whole present system.[14]

Marx was saying that the only answer to the fragmentation of the proletariat is the destruction of the present relations of production, vaguely connecting this with political organization. However the question remains as to the role that political organization must play in order for the proletariat to carry out its political tasks and the precise relation of this political organization to the class.

Marx's scanty coverage of this issue was somewhat increased by a letter he wrote a few months before the Paris Commune. In the middle of his battle with Bakunin, Marx openly identified the *class* movement with an expressly *political* movement.

> [E]very movement in which the working class as a *class* confronts the ruling classes and tries to constrain them from without is a political movement. For instance, the attempts by strikes, etc., in a particular factory or even in a particular trade to compel individual capitalists to reduce the working day, is a purely economic movement. On the other hand the movement to force through an eight-hour, etc., *law* is a *political* movement. And in this way out of the separate economic movements of the workers there grows up everywhere a *political* movement, that is to say, a *class* movement with the object of enforcing its interests in a general form, in a form possessing general, socially coercive force. While these movements presuppose a certain degree of previous organization, they are in turn equally a means of developing this organization.[15]

This passage is important because Marx clearly stated the necessity of political organization for class action on the part of the proletariat. However, Marx persisted in seeing the political movement as a natural outgrowth of other struggles of the working class. He saw politics as unifying the proletariat but he did not see that this function of unity itself, combined with the characteristic separation of the political and economic under capitalism, could engender an independent, *representative* relationship between the proletariat and its protagonists.

There is one final example of Marx's sporadic awareness that the proletariat does not automatically and immediately constitute itself as a class actor. It is remarkable because it is one of the very few instances in which Marx explicitly ascribed a positive role to moral appeals.

> Saint Sancho [Stirner] again presents the proletarians here as a "closed society", which has only to take the decision of "seizing" in order the next day to put a summary end to the entire hitherto existing world order. But in reality the proletarians arrive at this unity only through a long process of development in which the appeal to their right also plays a part. Incidentally, this appeal to their right is only a means of making them take shape as 'they', as a revolutionary, united mass.[16]

Again Marx considered this development to be essentially unproblematic and assigned no role to an organization. On the other hand, Lenin's assumed intimate relation between party and class was to be tested by taking power and attempting to actually construct socialism.

The major problem with Marx's predominant conception of the proletariat is simply that the working class is not naturally homogeneous nor unified. This necessitates a specifically political organization of the proletariat in order for it to act as a class. Because of its function of unity, there is a tendency for this organization to attain an autonomous existence above the class, i.e. to develop a representative relation to the class.

There are many bases for the generation of an autonomous political organization of the working class. For example, skill levels persist, even though Marx was correct about the tendency of capitalism to reduce skill differentiation. (This was supported in a study by Harry Braverman.)[17] Engels himself noted the persistence of skill levels in 1885 although he argued, again persuasively, that "skilled" is often a mere designation assigned by craft union rules.[18] It is not actually "skill" which remains but the relatively favorable market position of workers who attain the designation "skilled". Nonetheless, this differing market position is a continuing source of disunity which Marx and Engels generally underestimated.

On a broader level, a capitalist economy can be ordered such that objective contradictions within the class surface. For example, the economy of

162

the United States is divided into three sectors: large capital, small capital, and the state sector.[19] The large capital sector has some measure of control over its markets, thereby enabling it to pay its workers higher wages and benefits. The small capital sector firms, on the other hand, as suppliers to large capital firms and functioning in a more competitive environment, operate with smaller profit margins and cannot pay high wages. Because of the dependence of small capital on large capital, the high wages of workers in the latter are partly a result of low wages of workers in the former. Since small capital firms employ disproportionately more women, blacks, and other 'minorities', the relation between small capital sector workers and large capital sector workers becomes charged with other divisive issues. This is an example of a structural contradiction within the working class that has severe consequences for the possibility of *class* action.

What is true domestically is even more apparent in the international sphere. Engels saw this in regard to English workers (1882):

> You ask me what the English workers think about colonial policy. Well, exactly the same as they think about politics in general: the same as the bourgeois think. There is no workers' party here, there are only Conservatives and Liberal-Radicals, and the workers are cheerfully consuming their share of England's monopoly of the world market and the colonies.[20]

Marx and Engels knew that any workers' movement must be international if it is to be successful, therefore this is a terrible and pressing source of weakness. Unfortunately, on the whole they underestimated the persistence of exclusive national interests of the proletariats of different countries. What was said of English workers could be said in their turn of American workers and, perhaps, Japanese workers. Needless to say, the more or less conscious collusion of large sectors of the labor force in imperialist policies is of long standing.

In addition to these specific domestic and international structural problems of the proletariat there is a much more basic, one might say 'ontological', disunity of the proletariat which exacerbates the other divisions. The proletariat must be conceived just as it is, existing in an in-dividualized exchange society with the "terrifyingly real" consequence of *competition.* In this situation, contrary to a major assumption of Marx, the interests of the individual proletarian and the proletarian class do not coincide, especially in the short run.

The primary interest of the individual worker is not to abolish classes. The interest of the individual worker is to escape his or her class. As Mihaly Vajda has argued, the only situation in which the individual proletarian interest and the class interest, *and* the long-term and short-term interests, coincide is when the workers are in the most desperate poverty.

> A unified proletarian "interest" has never existed. It has never been the case that every single proletarian could lose only his chains and nothing else. I do not say that the use of *the* proletarian interest as an abstraction -- as an analogy of the similarly abstract bourgeois interest -- is unjustified. But a group only aspires to enforce the *Gesamtinteresse* which does not coincide with the private interests of its members when the non-enforcement of it would universally hinder the realization of the private interest of the members of the group. ... Hence we must suppose that the proletariat will enforce its "*Gesamtinteresse*", i.e. overthrow capitalism, only if without such enforcement its elementary vital conditions (the elementary vital conditions of the society as a whole) would be imperilled. Only, that is to say, if capitalism were in a permanent state of crisis and impasse which would universally threaten the vital conditions of humanity.[21]

Aside from the 'straw-man' aspects of his argument ("every single proletarian"), Vajda indicates precisely what Marx assumed: an intractable crisis which identifies the individual and class interest, the short-term and long-term interests. Although one can debate whether capitalism is in a permanent state of crisis, the fact remains that these economic difficulties have not had the effect of unifying the proletariat but rather have intensified intraclass competition.

The basic problem of the proletariat is that the isolation of the individual worker is *real*. The proletarian is born of bourgeois conditions and suffers the same problems of unity as the bourgeoisie. As Marx argued in *The German Ideology*, the major conceptual difference between a 'class' and an 'Estate' is precisely that the former lacks the community and immediate political expression of the latter. Marx was very clear on this in his analysis of the bourgeoisie; because of its isolation (competition) and the division of economic and political spheres, the bourgeoisie is forced to develop independent political organizations, in this case a state. Marx did not believe

164

this to be true of the proletariat because of its dire straits (unifying the individual and class, long-term and short-term interests) and because they are 'associated' by their particular role in the productive process (urban, factory concentration, trade unions, etc.).

However, Marx was in error. The proletariat cannot achieve self-activity because *it is a 'class' in the precise sense of the term, just like the bourgeoisie.* Marx too easily brushed aside the terrible effects of the individual worker's position in capitalist production. His many assertions of the "atomization"[22] or even "dot-like isolation"[23] of the proletarians must be taken seriously. The proletariat is indeed "alienated".

Marx argued this point very eloquently in all of his works: in the discussion of the debilitating effects of the division of labor (especially the separation of mental and material labor) in *The Economic and Philosophic Manuscripts of 1844* and in *The German Ideology*, and in the complementary discussion of the general "brutalization" of the worker under capitalism in the *Grundrisse* and *Capital.*[24] Marx was too persuasive in these works for us to simply disregard them when we turn to the possibility of self-emancipation of the proletariat.

Too many theorists would have it both ways: that the proletariat is "alienated" and subject to "fetishism" yet somehow can overcome this by its own resources and achieve self-emancipation. One Marxist who rejected such an easy answer to this dilemma was Antonio Gramsci:

> To expect masses who are reduced to such conditions of bodily and spiritual slavery to express their own autonomous historical will; to expect them spontaneously to initiate and sustain a revolutionary action -- this is purely an illusion on the part of the ideologues.[25]

The separation of workers from one another by the division of labor and by the intra-class competition resulting from exchange relations is real. In a great many ways the proletariat is as isolated as the peasantry and has a similar need for political representation in order to counteract its 'urban idiocy'.

Marx did not fully appreciate the essential disunity of the proletariat because, like so many after him, he identified the proletariat especially by its relation to the means of production, i.e. its position in the sphere of production. Although this is useful, unless one also notes the position of the proletariat in the sphere of circulation/exchange one will not see some of its basic characteristics. The real existence of the working class, the way its members live and act, is the only basis for comprehending its possibilities for historical action for its class objectives. Marx underestimated the fragmenting effects of the worker's position in circulation and even the fragmentation it suffers because of its position in the capitalist division of labor.

There is another basis of the disunity of the proletariat that must be given weight equal to the economic bases: the representative state itself. In my discussion of Marx's critique of Hegel's political philosophy I noted Marx's early understanding of the shortcomings of the democratic republic. At the time Marx was reaching for a comprehensive critique of representative politics in general based on the argument that the formalism of representative democracy disrupts the community, or at the very least maintains its fragmentation.[26]

However, most Marxian theory provides little guidance for criticism of representative democracy and classical Marxian discussion of the issue is the least satisfying aspect of Marxism, and the most historically dated. As Goran Therborn noted:

> It is not surprising that the classical Marxian writers produced almost nothing of substance on the question, for none of them had personal experience of a fully-fledged bourgeois democracy.[27]

It is quite reasonable that Marx did not fully understand the deleterious effects of the democratic state on the proletariat.

Actually Marx and Engels were in certain situations quite hopeful about the use of universal suffrage for advancing working class political power. For example, Marx once stated that

> universal suffrage is the equivalent of political power for the working class of England, where the proletariat forms the large majority of the population, where, in the long, though underground, civil war, it has gained a clear consciousness of its position as a class ...[28]

As is well-known, Marx once suggested the same about the United States and Holland.[29] Engels went so far as to argue that "the democratic republic is even the specific form of the dictatorship of the proletariat," and this *after* the Paris Commune and the thesis of the 'smashing' of the state.[30]

However for the most part Marx and Engels did not hold illusions nor make broad statements about universal suffrage and parliamentary politics to promote the workers' cause was usually argued in the context of concrete circumstances. Marx and Engels never forgot that Louis Bonaparte was elected by universal suffrage.[31]

Recent theory has gone far beyond Marx's misgivings about modern democracy to argue that *by its practical and ideological structure* the representative democratic state contributes to the disunity of the proletariat. Participation in existing democracies has often been regarded by Marxists as an ideological device for giving workers the illusion of freedom, equality, and opportunity. A more advanced view, presented for example by Lukacs in *Lenin,* asserts the usefulness of democratic ideology for actively disorganizing the working class by 'individualizing' its members.[32] One of the purposes of 'bourgeois' democracy is:

> preventing the formation of an independent ideology among the oppressed classes of the population which would correspond to their own class interests; of binding the individual members of these classes as single individuals, as mere 'citizens', to an abstract state reigning over and above all classes; of *disorganizing these classes as classes* and pulverizing them into atoms easily manipulated by the bourgeoisie.[33]

This presentation is quite similar to the argument made by the young Marx against the 'abstract individual' in his analysis of Hegel's political philosophy.[34]

Lukacs' discussion and others like it are persuasive if we do not think of ideology as 'mere fancies or beliefs' in people's heads. If we view ideas as in some way structurally related to practice, as determined and determining in turn,[35] rather than regarding ideas as a mere reflex of practice, then Lukacs' argument about the disorganizing effects of democratic ideology has some force.

One of the enduring difficulties of Marxian theory is the relation of ideas to practice. Marx was particularly unhelpful in this regard by insisting in his famous preface to *A Contribution to the Critique of Political Economy* that "consciousness is determined by social being." This fosters the perspective of an absolute separation and causal relation between social practice and consciousness of that practice. Marx may not have intended this, but this has been its effect.

Lukacs and others have challenged this conception. Mihaly Vajda, a former student of Lukacs, has proposed that Lukacs' belief that ideas are real determinants of action is precisely his greatest contribution to Marxian theory.

> Lukacs is absolutely convinced of the fact that consciousness is just as constitutive of the world as its so-called material moments. The world of man is the world of human nexuses, and the latter cannot exist without consciousness as their factor.[36]

For this reason Lukacs' analyses often appear 'Hegelian' or 'idealist'. His argument about democratic ideology depends upon taking the ideas people hold seriously as at least co-determinants of actions.

Other Marxian theorists have pressed this conception of ideology as having a real, autonomous effect by referring to ideology as a "material practice".[37] Louis Althusser, Nicos Poulantzas, and others, elaborating on comments of Engels in letters (from the late 1880s until his death) on the autonomous determinations of ideology, have also argued the independent effects of ideological structures on class struggles.[38]

Regardless of one's *specific* conception of the effects of ideology on practice, if one acknowledges that ideology *does* have an effect, then traditional representative-democratic ideology is one of the bases of disunity of the proletariat. The representative tivetivedemocratic state establishes both workers and members of the bourgeoisie as individuals endowed with equal voting rights and importance, thereby obstructing class identification in the political sphere. This individualization, corresponding to the isolation of exchange relations, reinforces the separation of polity and economy by establishing the state as the unifier of this body of individuals/citizens.[39]

A concomitant of the representation of individuals is the minimization of political participation. As Erik Olin Wright has said,

> Perhaps the most important way by which the structure of the democratic capitalist state atomizes the working class is by limiting popular political life to voting, to periodically casting a ballot as private individuals for political representatives.[40]

Ernest Mandel, in noting the same isolation and consequent limitation of political participation, states that this is reinforced by the "reprivatization of leisure activities," e.g. community-weakening leisure such as television and the private automobile.[41]

Above all, however, Perry Anderson has given the most probing criticism of the effect of 'bourgeois' democracy on the working class. He not only agrees that representative democracy is fragmenting, he states that it is the *key* to bourgeois domination.

> [T]he economic divisions within the 'citizenry' are masked by the juridical parity between exploiters and exploited, and with them the complete *separation* and *non-participation* of the masses in the work of parliament. This separation is then constantly presented and represented to the masses as the ultimate incarnation of liberty: 'democracy' as the terminal point of history. The existence of the parliamentary state thus constitutes the formal framework of all other ideological mechanisms of the ruling class. It provides the general code in which every specific message elsewhere is transmitted. The code is all the more powerful because the juridical rights of citizenship are not a mere mirage: on the contrary, the civic freedoms and suffrages of bourgeois democracy are a tangible reality, whose completion was historically in part the work of the labor movement itself and whose loss would be a momentous defeat for the working class.[42]

For this reason Anderson calls representative democracy the "ideological lynchpin of Western capitalism."[43] Cultural controls, e.g. media, churches, and political parties, only perform a "complementary role".[44]

The great strength of the above argument is that it focuses on political structure in explaining the quiescence of the working class. Politics therefore becomes a determining moment in the possible transformation of society. This argument is far preferable to the sterile discussion of 'false consciousness'.

Anderson's work is particularly important and persuasive because he fully understands that bourgeois democracy presents the working class with a *real dilemma* that cannot be wished away by simplistic anti-parliamentarism. He underlines the necessity of imagining political forms which are not simply copies of bourgeois democracy, i.e. he indicates just how radical Marx's vision of the transcendence of the state is and what it entails.

The fragmentation of the proletariat by exchange relations, by the capitalist division of labor, and by the representative democratic state makes it impossible for the proletariat to form itself into a class subject. Like the bourgeoisie and the peasantry, the proletariat is a 'class' in the precise sense and in order to act on its class interests it must produce an autonomous "political dimension", i.e. it must be 'represented'.

Although a homogeneous working class does not exist, we need not take the viewpoint of Mihaly Vajda who, on this ground, rejects the notion of class politics altogether.

> [T]he homogeneous proletariat -- which is alleged to be theoretically existent in spite of its "apparent" dividedness, in spite of its dissolution into interest groups, and which came to be theoretically existent because such an entity is *necessary* to transcend the given society -- does not exist in reality. Consequently, all the forces which act as the representatives of this homogeneous class act with a false consciousness.[45]

Contrary to Vajda, even though a homogeneous class does not exist, *class relations do*. A party that works to destroy these relations 'represents' a class even if no homogeneous class subject exists.

The 'representation' of the working class has historically been manifested in both the creation of communist parties and in the existing socialist states. Representation by political parties is not as difficult an issue as representation by socialist states because communist parties in capitalist states must correspond somewhat to working class expectations or they will not have any followers. This was pointed out by Jean-Paul Sartre:

> The C. P. enjoys an authority which resembles that of a government; but since it doesn't have *institutions*, its sovereignty comes from the masses themselves. ... if the masses suddenly refused to follow it, it would lose everything; as powerful as it is, it resembles Antaeus, who had strength only when he was touching the earth.[46]

The only thing that can actually be discussed is whether the communist parties are *properly* representing the working class. The case of representation by existing socialist states, however, is of a different order because workers have no alternative to obedience to their commands.

As Etienne Balibar has argued, the forces which fragment the proletariat can ultimately be overcome only by the taking of political power by the working class.

> [T]he process of constitution of the proletariat as a class is ... an *unfinished* process, counteracted by the very capitalism which sets it in motion. This process precisely cannot be brought to a conclusion *without the proletarian revolution*: the proletariat can only finally complete its constitution *as a class* in so far as it succeeds in constituting itself *as the ruling class*, through the dictatorship of the proletariat. But this suggests that the dictatorship of the proletariat must itself be a contradictory situation, in a new sense: a situation in which the proletariat can finally succeed in overcoming its divisions and form itself into a class, yet in which at the same time it begins to cease to be a class to the extent that it ceases to suffer exploitation.[47]

The socialist state is necessary because the proletariat, like the bourgeoisie, cannot be constituted as a class subject without the mediation of its institutions. However the socialist state is a *proletarian* 'state' only to the extent that the 'state' actually takes measures to abolish classes. Classes can only be abolished by the absorption of state functions through real 'socialization' of the means of production and by the abolition of the division of labor. Therefore the socialist state can only realize the interests of the proletariat by creating conditions that make a state superfluous.

I have argued that the destruction of the 'representative' character of the state is the meaning of the 'transcendence of the state'. For Marx, the crux of the transcendence of the state is that state functions are no longer performed by an institution that stands in a separate and superior relation to society. Therefore the structures that engender representation are precisely those that need to be eliminated by the transitional regime. Its success in eliminating these structures is actually what defines it as a 'transitional' regime.

The problem of representation can be generalized in this manner: the more unified a body, the less independence possessed by its delegates. The transcendence of the state depends upon the possibility of creating a community such that the function of unity of the central coordinating apparatus is at least reduced to a minimum. This community can only be created by the abolition of those conditions of fragmentation which result from class society. In the next chapter I will expand the discussion of one of the key sources of fragmentation: the division of labor.

1. Georg Lukacs, "Towards a Methodology of the Problem of Organization," in *History and Class Consciousness* (Cambridge: MIT Press, 1973), p. 330.

2. Ibid., p. 315.

3. Ibid., pp. 326-327.

4. Lenin, "The Immediate Tasks of the Soviet Government" [April 28, 1918], in *Selected Works in Three Volumes* Volume 2 (New York: International Publishers, 1967), p. 668. See also Lenin, "'Left-Wing' Communism -- An Infantile Disorder," in ibid., Volume 3, p. 362.

5. See Lukacs' portrayal of Lenin's conception of the party: "Chapter Three: The Vanguard Party of the Proletariat," in *Lenin: A Study on the Unity of His Thought* (Cambridge: The MIT Press, 1974), pp. 24-38. Lukacs was hardly the 'elitist' that Lichtheim claims [George Lichtheim, *Georg Lukacs* (New York: Viking Press, 1970), p. 47]. Lukacs' notion of "imputed consciousness" is a heuristic device for charting the possible courses of the proletariat, to aid the party in its planning. It performs a function similar to Weber's "ideal type", from which it was derived.

6. For the former see Erik Olin Wright, *Class, Crisis, and the State* (London: New Left Books, 1978), p. 98 footnote, p. 102 footnote, and passim on "class capacities" as founded on the level of social structures, not political structures. For the latter see Santiago Carrillo, *Eurocommunism and the State* (Westport, CN: Lawrence Hill and Co., 1978).

7. Perry Anderson, "The Antinomies of Antonio Gramsci," *New Left Review* Number 100 (November 1976-January 1977), p. 27.

8. Ibid., p 27. This article serves as a self-critique by Anderson: see p. 27, footnote 48.

9. Ibid., pp. 45-46.

10. Marx and Engels, "The Manifesto of the Communist Party," in *The Revolutions of 1848: Political Writings Volume I*, edited and introduced by David Fernbach (New York: Random House, 1974), p. 87. See also ibid., p. 79 and Marx, *The Poverty of Philosophy* (New York: International Publishers, 1973) p. 125.

11. Marx, "The Alleged Splits in the International," in *The First International and After: Political Writings Volume III*, edited and introduced by David Fernbach (New York: Random House, 1974), p. 298. See also Marx, letter to Kugelmann (October 9, 1866), in *Marx-Engels Selected Correspondence* (Moscow: Progress Publishers, 1975), p. 172.

12. Marx and Engels, "The German Ideology," in *Marx-Engels Collected Works* Volume 5 (New York: International Publishers, 1976), p. 77. See also Georg Lukacs, "The Marxism of Rosa Luxemburg," in *History and Class Consciousness*, p. 41.

13. Marx and Engels, "The Manifesto," p. 76.

14. Marx and Engels, "The German Ideology," pp. 371-372.

15. Marx, letter to Bolte (November 23, 1871), in *Marx-Engels Selected Correspondence*, pp. 254-255. See also Marx and Engels, "The Manifesto," p. 76.

16. Marx and Engels, "The German Ideology," p. 323.

17. Harry Braverman, *Labor and Monopoly Capital* (New York: Monthly Review Press, 1974).

18. Engels, letter to Bebel (October 28, 1885), in *Marx-Engels Selected Correspondence*, pp. 364-365.

19. See Robert T. Averitt, *The Dual Economy* (New York: W. W. Norton and Co., Inc., 1968), and John Kenneth Galbraith, *Economics and the Public Purpose* (Boston: Houghton Mifflin Co., 1973).

20. Engels, letter to Kautsky (September 12, 1882), in *Marx-Engels Selected Correspondence*, pp. 330-331.

21. Mihaly Vajda, "The Myth and Reality of Mediation," in *The State and Socialism: Political Essays* (London: Allison and Busby, 1981), p. 18. Vajda's argument is very similar to that of Mancur Olson, Jr., in *The Logic of Collective Action* (New York: Schocken Books, 1971). For a different view on the same see Georg Lukacs' fascinating essay, "The Role of Morality in Communist Production," in *Tactics and Ethics: Political Essays 1919-1929* (New York: Harper and Row, Publishers, 1972), pp. 48-52.

22. Specifically in regard to the isolation of the worker in the modern workplace Marx once said: "he himself exists as an animated individual punctuation mark, as its [the machine's] living accessory." *Grundrisse*, translated and introduced by Martin Nicolaus (New York: Vintage Books, 1973), p. 470. See also Marx, *Capital* Volume 1 (New York: International Publishers, 1974), p. 92.

23. Marx, *Grundrisse*, p. 485.

24. Ibid., pp. 286-287. See also Marx, *Capital* Volume 1, Chapter X.

25. Antonio Gramsci, "Address to the Anarchists" [April 1920], in *Selections From Political Writings 1910-1920* (New York: International Publishers, 1977), p. 189.

26. Marx, "A Contribution to the Critique of Hegel's Philosophy of Right," in *Karl Marx: Early Writings*, introduced by Lucio Colletti (New York: Vintage Books, 1975), p. 132 and pp. 142-143.

27. Goran Therborn, "The Rule of Capital and the Rise of Democracy," *New Left Review* Number 103 (May-June 1977), p. 4.

28. Marx, "The Chartists," in *Surveys From Exile: Political Writings Volume II*, edited and introduced by David Fernbach (New York: Random House, 1974), p. 264.

29. Marx, "Speech on the Hague Congress," in *The First International and After*, p. 324.

30. Engels commenting on the Erfurt Programme of 1891, in *Writings on the Paris Commune (Marx-Engels)*, edited and introduced by Hal Draper (New York: Monthly Review Press, 1971), p. 235. For comments similar to these by Engels, see Engels, letter to Bernstein (January 1, 1884), in ibid., p. 345; and Engels, letter to Lafargue (March 6, 1894), in ibid., p. 447.

31. In February 1865 Engels expressed a like view on universal suffrage in Germany: "The Prussian Military Question and the German Workers' Party," in *The First International and After*, p. 142.

32. Lukacs, *Lenin*, p. 66.

33. Ibid., p. 66.

34. Marx, "Critique of Hegel's Philosophy of Right," p. 83 and p. 134.

35. A more interesting possibility is that beliefs are a part of the very definition of an 'action', a notion that cannot be explored here. See the works of Alasdair MacIntyre, John Plamenatz, Richard Bernstein, and G. E. M. Anscombe.

36. Vajda, "The Myth and Reality of Mediation," p. 32.

37. Erik Olin Wright, *Class, Crisis, and the State*, p. 38.

38. Louis Althusser, "Ideology and Ideological State Apparatuses," in *Lenin and Philosophy and Other Essays* (New York: Monthly Review Press, 1971), pp. 127- 186. Nicos Poulantzas, *Political Power and Social Classes* (London: New Left Books, 1973), pp. 206-207.

39. See Poulantzas, ibid., pp. 130-134 and pp. 276-277; Poulantzas, *State, Power, Socialism* (London: New Left Books/Verso, 1978), pp. 70-71. See also Anderson, op. cit., p. 28.

40. Wright, *Class, Crisis, and the State*, p. 245 and p. 102 footnote. See also Anderson, op. cit., p. 28.

41. "Ernest Mandel: A Political Interview," *New Left Review* Number 100 (November 1976-January 1977), p. 109.

42. Anderson, op. cit., p. 28.

43. Ibid., p. 28.

44. Ibid., p. 29.

45. Vajda, "The Myth and Reality of Mediation," p. 30.

46. Jean-Paul Sartre, *The Communists and Peace* [1952-1954] (New York: George Braziller, Inc., 1968), p. 65.

47. Etienne Balibar, *The Dictatorship of the Proletariat* (London: New Left Books, 1977), pp. 86-87. See also Lukacs' identical position: "The Marxism of Rosa Luxemburg," p. 41.

Chapter 10

Prospects for the Abolition of the Division of Labor

Besides the ability of the proletariat to escape the dialectic of political representation, the other key to Marx's hopes for the establishment of stateless society is the capacity of the transitional regime to abolish the division of labor. Although by politicizing the relations of production all socialist societies create the abstract possibility of restructuring production, this possibility has not been realized. Even in the critiques of 'actually existing socialism' it is quite remarkable how little attention is given to altering the structure of production.[1] Rather most criticism emphasizes purely political, e.g. traditional democratic (representative or otherwise), solutions to problems. This will not suit our purposes. By definition, to seriously consider the prospects for the transcendence of the state we must go beyond purely political answers.

Lucio Lombardo Radice recently argued that any hope for change in existing socialist societies demands that political transformation and economic transformation be "mapped out" together. Otherwise,

> efforts at liberalization and/or democratization are doomed to failure, as the fundamental historical experience of the Twentieth Congress has shown.[2]

Nicos Poulantzas even claimed that the thesis of the "smashing" of the state was extended by Lenin to the "smashing" of the "economic apparatus".[3] Although Poulantzas surely exaggerated in the case of Lenin, it is true that the complete transformation of the structure of production is a part, however underdeveloped, of the classics of Marxism. As the *Il Manifesto* group once noted, "it is an illusion to believe that socialism is a productive system inherited from capitalism with self-government added to it."[4]

Marx always argued that the primary productive structure that must be transformed for the development of full communism and stateless society is the 'division of labor'. On the basis of Marx's discussion in *The German Ideology* I have indicated that there is an intimate conceptual relation between "division of labor", "class conditions", and "classes". The abolition of the division of labor is simultaneously the abolition of class conditions and therefore is the ultimate determinant of the abolition of classes.

178

However we must explore in greater detail the prospects for the abolition of the division of labor and the manner in which it is simply a broader way of saying 'abolition of classes'.

Hardly any aspect of the theory of the transcendence of the state has come under more ready attack than the idea that the division of labor can be abolished, especially under modern conditions of production. Various critics have concentrated in particular on the 'hunter, fisherman, critical critic' passage in *The German Ideology* and respond that, although this flexibility of individuals may be possible in a simple society of only broad occupations such as 'fishing', it is impossible in an advanced society. A person cannot be a neurosurgeon in the morning, a ballerina in the afternoon, and a logical positivist after dinner.[5] Marx's proposed abolition of the division of labor only applies (if at all) to primitive economies. Specialization may be the plague of modern man but it is also the necessary basis for progress.

The idea that the division of labor cannot be abolished and therefore the state is necessary for unifying social functions is not the sole province of anti-socialist thinkers. As Rudolf Bahro has reported:

> In most countries of 'actually existing socialism' ... it is precisely the trained ideologists who generally have only an ironic laugh, in private, for such 'illusions' as that of the abolition of the division of labor, or an end to relations of domination and the state.[6]

Even Milovan Djilas, a former leader of Yugoslavia, a favorite country of proponents of the transcendence of the state, rejects the idea that the state can be transcended, partly on the ground that it is necessary for the "uniting of its [society's] various functions."[7]

Marx responded firmly that specialization based on the rigorous differentiation of task is actually a part of an earlier stage of capitalism. In the period of 'manufacture' the productive process was broken down into its constituent elements and laborers were assigned more and more simple 'detail functions'. However the succeeding 'industrial' period reaped the benefits of the developments of the period of manufacture. The atomization of the productive process made it possible to introduce machines to perform the detail functions. The tendency of capitalism is to reduce the role of the worker to mere 'machine-tender' and this reveals itself in the decline in the need for skilled labor.[8]

For Marx, therefore, the differentiation of task is not so complex as it first appears. Although there are a bewildering number of branches of a modern economy, the vast majority of positions in those branches are quite similar to each other. Monitoring a machine in a large insurance office is not that much different from monitoring a machine in an automobile factory. It is true that as new industries emerge there is again a necessity for skilled labor but the general tendency for the reduction of skills asserts itself as the industry matures. A perfect example is the computer industry which a few years ago required highly trained personnel. Now that the various aspects of production have been separated, relatively little training is needed for most of the tasks.[9]

Therefore the remark with regard to 'neurosurgery' is correct but the inference is not. The vast majority of places in a modern economy do not require the expertise of neurosurgery. The necessity of specialization only applies to a small part of the occupations of society. The constant cries for 'experienced' personnel is most likely an attempt to save marginal training costs, the importance of which will be reduced in a society with different priorities. Confinement of individuals to one task is a political problem, not a technical one.

Z. A. Jordan has rejected this defense of Marx by arguing that Marx himself later rejected the idea of the abolition of the division of labor. Jordan says that *The German Ideology* is corrected by the passage in *Capital* Volume 3 in which Marx said that work will always be part of "the realm of necessity". Instead of the abolition of the division of labor as the basis for realizing individuality, the mature Marx recognized that only non-work time, leisure time, can be the realm of freedom. As Marx stated:

> In fact the realm of freedom actually begins only where labor which is determined by necessity and mundane considerations ceases; thus in the very nature of things it lies beyond the sphere of actual material production. ... Freedom in this field can only consist in socialized man, the associated producers, rationally regulating their interchange with nature, bringing it under their common control, instead of being ruled by it as by the blind forces of Nature; and achieving this with the least expenditure of energy and under conditions most favorable to, and worthy of, their human nature. But it nonetheless still remains a realm of necessity. Beyond it begins that development of human energy which is an end in itself, the true realm of freedom, which,

180

however, can blossom forth only with this realm of necessity as its basis. The shortening of the working day is its basic prerequisite.[10]

This passage seems to be interpreted by Jordan to mean that the productive process cannot be changed in *any* substantial way, that it is simply a necessary evil.[11]

This passage certainly makes Marx's project more ambiguous. What he seems to be asserting is that, although "labor cannot become play, as Fourier would like,"[12] a *kind* of freedom *within* the realm of necessity can be achieved by restructuring the labor process is ways "favorable to, and worthy of, their human nature." Nevertheless, in this passage the real emphasis does seem to be on non-production time, the true realm of freedom.

Marx believed that capitalism itself creates the prerequisites sitessites-for expanding the 'realm of freedom' because it reduces the necessary labor-time to a minimum in the interest of increasing unpaid surplus-labor.[13] Under socialism the needs of people will increase above the minimum allowed by capitalism but production will also increase such that there will be an increase in free time. To underscore the point Marx quoted an earlier economist: "Truly wealthy a nation, when the working day is six rather than twelve hours."[14] For Marx, the final goal of any process of production, no matter how structured, is "wealth", which is "measured" by "disposable time".[15]

The above passages do indeed de-emphasize the abolition of the division of labor and cast some doubt on the commitment of the mature Marx to the radical transformation of production, instead of simply the minimization of its importance in determining the character of society. However in the *Grundrisse*, from which some of the above passages are culled, there are longer discussions of "wealth" and "potentialities" which actually weaken the entire distinction between the 'realm of necessity' and the 'realm of freedom' on which the above argument is based. First, Marx elaborated on his conception of "wealth":

> what is wealth other than the universality of human needs, capacities, pleasures, productive forces, etc., created through universal exchange? The full development of human mastery over the forces of nature, those of so-called nature as well of humanity's own nature? The absolute working out of his creative potentialities, with no presupposition other than the previous historic development, which

makes this totality of development, i.e. the development of all human powers as such the end in itself, not as measured on a *predetermined* yardstick? Where he does not reproduce himself in one specificity, but produces his totality? Strives not to remain something he has become, but is in the absolute movement of becoming?[16]

In another place in the *Grundrisse* Marx ascribed this development of the capacities of humanity not only to "disposable time" but to the *labor process itself*. Arguing against Adam Smith's conception of labor ("as a curse") Marx wrote:

Certainly, labor obtains its measure from the outside, through the aim to be attained and the obstacles to be overcome in attaining it. But Smith has no inkling whatever that this overcoming of obstacles is in itself a liberating activity -- and that, further, the external aims become stripped of the semblance of merely external natural urgencies, and become posited as aims which the individual himself posits -- hence as self-realization, objectification of the subject, hence real freedom, whose action is, precisely, labor. ... The work of material production can achieve this character only (1) when its social character is posited, [and] (2) when it is of a scientific and at the same time general character, not merely human exertion as a specifically harnessed natural force, but exertion as subject, which appears in the productive process not in a merely natural, spontaneous form, but as an activity regulating all the forces of nature.[17]

Following Hegel's discussion of "Lordship and Bondage",[18] Marx argued throughout his work that it is in *production*, in the labor process, that men and women actualize and extend their creative capacities, *or* find those same capacities stunted as under capitalism. Unless we are willing to disregard much of Marx's lifelong analyses of the labor process, we must *reject* (as I believe Engels did) the rigid distinction between the 'realm of necessity' and the 'realm of freedom' that Marx appears to make in the famous passage from *Capital*.[19] Both the process of production *and* "disposable time" allow the unfolding of man's creative potential, each favorable to the development of different *kinds* of capacities. Work need not necessarily be a burden, although it is quite likely that it can never become "play". On this basis we must insist on the centrality of the abolition of the division of labor for Marx's vision of communism.

To return to the specific topic under discussion, there are three different aspects of the division of labor which bear on the theory of the transcendence of the state: (1) the *general* confinement of individuals to one position in the division of labor, (2) the specific exclusion of the populace from positions of "mental labor", and (3) the difference between the division of labor *within a production unit* and the *social* division of labor.

The general confinement of individuals to one position in the division of labor is one of the most important sources of disunity in a society.[20] This fragmentation is alleviated somewhat if commodity production is abolished, reducing the pressures of the market which exacerbate competition among individuals. However, competition for resources will remain because of the particular interests, demands, and perspectives unique to each position in the productive process. Even a voluntary 'initial choice' of one's position in the division of labor cannot eliminate these forces of fragmentation and particularism.[21] Only variation of occupation can make the workforce as a whole sensitive to the special problems of different positions in production.

The major aspect of the division of labor which is important for the possibility of transcending the state, however, is the separation of "mental labor" from "material labor", or, more precisely, "planning/control" from "execution". Marx regarded the division of mental and material labor as the fundamental cleavage in the division of labor.

> Division of labor only becomes truly such from the moment when a division of material and mental labor occurs.[22]

Marx stated that this division can cause antagonism even within the bourgeoisie,[23] and argued throughout *The German Ideology* that it is this division which is ultimately the source of an idealist view of history.

In the process of production the separation of mental and material labor manifests itself as the separation of planning/control functions from execution by the concentration of the former in a 'management' separate from the rest of the workforce. As usual, critics of the theory of the transcendence of the state consider this separation as an eternal, technical necessity of modern production. Again, an appropriate response would be that although management *positions* may be necessary, a management *stratum* is not. Coordination of a differentiated labor process is logically distinct from the necessity for a professional management.

The separation of planning/control from execution in the productive process is one of the specific characteristics of capitalism, as revealed in the earlier discussion of the separation of the laborer from the control ('possession') and direction of production which he had under feudalism.[24] This separation intensified as capitalism progressed: more and more aspects of the direction of production were transferred to a centralized management. Harry Braverman has convincingly argued this tendency, relating it to the decrease in the requirement for skilled labor and also to class struggle in the workplace.[25] One of the primary goals behind the transformation of the labor process under capitalism was (and *is*) the destruction of the Saint-Simonian 'diffusion of power', based on the necessary knowledge of agents in production, by stripping most places in production of their directive functions. The epitome of this is, of course, 'Taylorism', which was explicitly embraced to reduce the power of workers over the process of production.[26]

One of the critical failures of Soviet society and others modelled on it is that they instituted such capitalist productive techniques, assuming that they are the most efficient. Corrigan et al. analyzed the relation between present Soviet society and the assumption of the Bolsheviks of the superiority and *neutrality* of these techniques.[27] They concluded quite rightly that by maintaining these techniques, which necessarily exclude the masses from participation in management (e.g. Lenin's notion of "one-man management", albeit founded on the expectation of workplace democracy),[28] Bolshevism obstructed alternatives which could have emerged to challenge the existence of the state.

However, we must be careful *how* we criticize these structures of production. The argument of Corrigan and his colleagues leads in the direction of the return of control decisions to the shop floor, i.e. to reversing the tendency of capitalism to completely separate control and execution in positions in the process of production. According to Corrigan, returning discretion over production to the shop floor will release

> the most fundamental of socialism's productive forces: the knowledge of better ways of making things locked up in communities of direct producers.[29]

It is true that alternative modes of production can only be freed by attacking the capitalist labor process and no doubt workers would have insight into such alternatives. However the separation of control and execution in positions in the productive process is actually an historic advance. The elimination of directive aspects of the majority of production positions was supported by Marx because reducing these places to *mere* execution makes it easier to mechanize these tasks. Attempting to alter the structure of labor process by reintegrating execution and control on the level of *places* in production would be a step backward, a new 'Luddite' movement based on an assumed superior knowledge of workers.

One cannot have it both ways: either the structure of capitalist production substantially destroys the knowledge of workers of production as a whole or it does not. The proposals of Corrigan et al. are mistakenly focused on *places* in production rather than the confinement of occupants *to* these places. Marx never argued for the reintegration of control and execution in positions of production. Rather he argued against forcing individuals to always remain in the same position. Rotation of task, not destruction of differentiation, was always his answer.

A trivial but oft-repeated objection (not least of all by workers themselves) to rotation in the occupation of positions of execution and control is that workers are intellectually incapable of directing production. That this is a mere rationalization of the existing state of affairs was pointed out by Adam Smith himself.

> The difference of natural talents in different men is, in reality, much less than we are aware of; and the very different genius which appears to distinguish men of different professions, when grown up to maturity, is not upon many occasions so much the cause as the effect of the division of labor.[30]

As Wright elaborated, this conception or 'ideology' is "embedded in the material practice" of the separation of control and execution in production.[31] Once most positions in production have been stripped of their directive aspects it is very simple to demonstrate the ignorance of the workers. Workers themselves reflect this belief in their inherent inability by what Rudolf Bahro calls the conscious behavior of "subalternity".[32]

There are two major consequences of the exclusion of workers from positions of planning/control which are relevant to the theory of the transcendence of the state. First, exclusion of the masses reproduces the basis of the state in the rule of "expertise". Acording to Bahro this is one of the oldest bases of the state 'in general'.[33] Throughout this work I have tried

to avoid Bahro's transhistorical conception of the state but it is certainly
true that the structural separation of positions of control and exclusion of
most workers from these positions serves as an additional basis for the
autonomy of the directive functions. However, unlike Bahro, I do not consider it a *sufficient* cause of the state; it merely reinforces the other bases I
have discussed. Nonetheless, it is a crucial basis that must be eliminated in
order to further the transcendence of the state.

A second consequence of the strict separation of the occupants of control positions from those of execution positions (and of mental and material
labor in general) is a psychological one mentioned by several Eastern
European theorists. The lack of control of workers over production en-
courages a demand for satisfaction through consumption of goods. As
Wlodzimierz Brus states it:

> disillusionment about the possibility of real influence on the general
> questions finds a natural outlet in a striving to make amends in private
> forms. In this way a mass of social energy is wasted.[34]

Bahro calls this phenomenon the generation of "compensatory interests"
which have a very strong hold on large sectors of the population.[35] This is
one of the causes of the intense desire in socialist societies for Western
goods and consumption patterns.

This is a particularly important issue because it forces us to reconsider
an essential aspect of the theory of the transcendence of the state: the
problem of the elimination of 'scarcity'. The overcoming of scarcity is crucial to the transcendence of the state and is part of the common definition
of 'full communism'. (Marx spoke of "abundance" but he meant substantially the same thing.) For example, the overcoming of scarcity is the central
assumption of Bertell Ollman's characterization of communism and his entire argument depends upon the possibility of its achievement.[36] 'Scarcity'
also has the greatest explanatory role in Sartre's theory of alienated social
structures in his *Critique of Dialectical Reason.*[37]

Scarcity is of course a major difficulty in attempts to build communism,
but again we must be careful how we conceive it. As much as it would
simplify things to conceptually eliminate it, 'scarcity' and 'needs' have a
subjective, i.e. psychological, dimension. Bahro and others recognize that
the *feeling* of 'scarcity' is hardly less 'material' than 'objective' scarcity
(which Marx also acknowledged as the "cultural" components of "subsis-

tence level")[38] and this 'feeling' of scarcity is intimately linked to the social structure of existing socialism.

According to Bahro and Brus, a real and effective feeling of scarcity is engendered by the exclusion of workers from participation in the direction of social processes and therefore from control over their lives. The common desire for Western-style consumption in existing socialist societies is psychological compensation for the impossibility of personality fulfillment through work and social relationships.

Bahro argues that these "compensatory interests" stand in the way of change in existing socialist societies by artificially maintaining 'scarcity'.

> Material insatiability costs us the freedom for higher development, subjects us to regulations which rest on compulsion, and gives society a step-motherly character. ... The compensatory desire and compulsion to possess, to use, to consume, has forced the continuation of a fight for production, in which we shall still be too poor for communism in a hundred years.[39]

The social structure must be reorganized in order to destroy the source of consumerism; socialist societies must reject what Corrigan et al. call the "fetish of the productive forces".[40] Bahro insists that the goal must not be the overtaking of the West's productive capacity but the fulfillment of the original promise of communism as an entirely different and higher civilization.[41] The *only* way to eliminate consumerism and the definition of 'scarcity' it engenders is to increase participation in the decision-making process by allowing workers access to directive positions.

Mihaly Vajda has argued a similar but broader conception with regard to one of the more liberal socialist states, Hungary. He asserts that cultural and economic liberalization of Hungary was consciously pursued by the authorities as a substitute for democratization of decision-making.

> This liberalization involved the implementation of a number of measures previously unheard of under the present form of socialism. In this way, *always provided they renounced all claim to participation in decision-making*, the life of the population was made considerably easier. Everyday life became what is commonly termed tolerable. As for the authorities too, liberalization bore fruit: the population, increasingly preoccupied by its private life and increasingly immersed in the isolation of the family, created increasingly

fewer [*sic*] problems for the authorities and above all no longer represented a threat. People settled down into apathy.[42]

However Vajda further argues that this situation is increasingly difficult to maintain: European socialist economies simply cannot sustain the consumption patterns they stimulate in the population by depriving them of meaningful political participation.

> Because totalitarian power denies human beings all social goals, it is forced to direct its efforts toward the personal interests of society's members. Indeed, the power apparatus must encourage consumerism in spite of an official ideology which condemns consumerism and in spite of an economic system which does not favor the production of consumer goods.[43]

Vajda concludes that the situation is inherently unstable, a position with which Brus agrees.[44]

For all of the reasons that Western-style consumption is encouraged -- consequence of the exclusion of workers from directive positions on all levels, political strategy of the ruling stratum, and political *necessity* of the ruling stratum -- the state in socialist societies is reinforced. As long as 'scarcity' exists, the state is justified as the necessary "hothouse" for the development of the productive forces.

The best possibility for eliminating the effects of the separation of mental and material labor still appears to be variation of occupation, or as Bahro restated it, "several individuals for each job, several jobs for each individual."[45] The end of specialization would have several consequences. Forced rotation would interest workers more in production than would mere democratic control of managers because it would give workers greater knowledge of the productive process as a whole, impossible under present conditions. In this way it would break down the "idiocy" of the worker and destroy "those conditions that produce subaltern individuals, a species of thinking ants, instead of a free people."[46] Greater knowledge of the population of production as a whole would severely restrict the ability of managers to assert autonomy under the guise of 'expertise'.

Secondly, it would increase production by liberating what Marx always considered the greatest productive force: free individuality.[47] It is this potential productive force of the well-rounded individual that is the basis of

Marx's assertion that a communist society is a society in which "the free development of each is the condition for the free development of all."[48]

Finally, variation of occupation of positions of control and execution would generally reduce the demands on production by 'deprivatizing' aspects of people's lives. Universal participation contains the promise of weakening the hold of "compensatory interests" which are ultimately founded in the *distinction* between a "realm of necessity" and a "realm of freedom". Only this will prove communism to be a different form of civilization, not simply more of the same.

Many proponents of the transcendence of the state have supported self-management socialism on the grounds that it is the most likely way of developing a community cohesive enough to reduce the function of unity and therefore the need for representation.tiontion However, once we commit ourselves to the development of self-management groups a new dimension of the division of labor reveals itself: the *social* division of labor.

Thus far we have only been concerned with the division of labor within a production unit. But different units have different roles in the process of production in society as a whole. When Marx discussed the abolition of the division of labor he had in mind primarily the division of labor within a factory. He frequently conceived socialist production as the creation of one, gigantic, society-wide, democratically-organized factory and specifically used the example of a factory as a division of labor without exchange, the first step toward communist production.[49]

However, once we leave the statist model behind, a practical and conceptual difference between the division of labor *within the workplace* and the division of labor *in society* emerges, i.e. differentiation of production tasks *among* production units. It is quite likely, as Kautsky argued, that these production units will become competitive for resources and corporate-minded or 'syndicalistic'.[50] Bahro more recently expressed the same doubts:

> The interests of the producers are particular interests among other
> particular interests, and as long as they have their pivot in producer
> cooperatives, they are therefore fundamentally incapable of produc-
> ing any plan that can satisfy the overall social requirement, no mat-
> ter how democratically they are synthesized from the bottom up-
> wards.[51]

If this is the case (and it has been asserted to be true in Yugoslavia),[52] then this is a new source for antagonisms and therefore for a representative institution embodying and enforcing community, above and apart from society.

Different solutions have been offered for this problem. Bahro suggests the creation of a new "League of Communists", i.e. a political party, to lead a "cultural revolution" against particularism.[53] Karl Korsch proposed a "consumers union" to bind together the interests of the whole society apart from the particular interests of production units.[54] All of these discussions are highly speculative in their present form.

Self-management socialism does seem to be the most promising form for experimentation in structuring the labor process and for involving workers in the process of production. However, as long as production units are the only available basis for creating a community cohesive enough to eliminate representation, and as long as these communities are not self-sufficient, then the need for a unifying center reasserts itself. In the context of developing a proletarian political party, Sartre argued that the distinction between the interests of the class and the interests and perspectives of self-management groups results in a "duality of power".

> This means an open and irreducible relation between the *unitary* moment, which falls to the political organization of the class, and the moments of self-government, the councils, the fused groups. I insist on that word "irreducible" because there can only be a permanent tension between the two moments.[55]

The same must be said of the socialist polity. If we insist on the importance of self-management structures -- and there does not seem to be any alternative at present -- then we cannot avoid a higher coordinating body which performs the function of unity through macroeconomic planning and provides an arena for decisions on incomparable choices (e.g. investment versus consumption).

However, the distance of this realm from production units can be decreased by restructuring production. The abolition of the division of labor in the workplace which produces greater knowledge of individuals and real participation on one level can at least result in a countervailing power, or a "situation of dual supremacy".[56] Institution of the measures of the Paris Commune of 1871, where appropriate (limitations of terms of office, immediate recall, etc.), will also bind the national coordinating apparatus to the units of production. In the final analysis, however, this basis for political representation cannot be eliminated, only circumscribed.

Marx and Engels supported the abolition of the division of labor for more reasons than simply to encourage the transcendence of the state. In their conception the abolition of the division of labor is also the abolition of 'classes' in both senses in which the term has been used in this work: (1) a particular relation to the means of production and (2) a social structure which isolates and limits individuals by their position in the productive process.

Marx always considered 'classes' to be primarily structures of alienation and therefore crucially related to the other two structures of alienation, the division of labor and property. In one passage he and Engels made this connection explicit:

> the class ... assumes an independent existence as against the individuals, so that the latter find their conditions of life predetermined, and have their position in life and hence their personal development assigned to them by their class, thus being subsumed under it. This is the same phenomenon as the subjection of the separate individuals to the division of labor and can only be removed by the abolition of private property and of labor itself.[57]

The abolition of the division of labor is therefore simultaneously the abolition of classes and property.

This is underscored by Marx and Engels' conception of property in *The German Ideology*, which they called "the power of disposing of the labor-power of others."[58] In this phrase Marx and Engels clearly showed what is ultimately entailed by the abolition of classes and the achievement of communism: the elimination of 'property' is the elimination of a certain kind of 'power'. The goal of communism is the establishment of a productive process that "gives no one domination."[59]

This is contrasted to the previous mode of production by the frequent use of political metaphors in the description of the productive process of capitalism: "the lords of capital", "wage-slavery", etc. Communism, on the other hand, is the redistribution of power in production by the restructuring of the relations of production. It is *not*, contemporary historical experience notwithstanding, simply the absorption of property into the "crystalline structure of the state."[60]

The abolition of classes is the abolition of power relations in production and this is only accomplished by the abolition of the permanent confinement of the majority to powerless positions in production. In this way alone is communism the collective control of the "associated individuals" of their "life expression". Therefore communism can only be achieved by the abolition of the division of labor.

192

1. The notable exception to this is of course Rudolf Bahro, *The Alternative in Eastern Europe* (London: New Left Books/Verso, 1978). For a brief review of critiques of existing socialism see Lucio Lombardo Radice, "State Socialism," in *Rudolf Bahro: Critical Responses*, edited by Ulf Wolter (White Plains, NY: M. E. Sharpe, Inc., 1980), pp. 129-151.

2. Radice, "State Socialism," p. 136.

3. Nicos Poulantzas, *Fascism and Dictatorship* (London: New Left Books, 1974), p. 304.

4. In an interview with Jean-Paul Sartre by *Il Manifesto*, "Masses, Spontaneity, Party," in *The Socialist Register 1970*, edited by Ralph Miliband and John Saville (London: Merlin Press, 1970), p. 243.

5. See Walter Z. Laqueur, "Introduction," *Survey* Number 38 (October 1961), p. 9; Bertram D. Wolfe, *One Hundred Years in the Life of a Doctrine* (New York: Dial Press, 1965), p. 335; Alec Nove, *The Economics of Feasible Socialism* (London: George Allen and Unwin, 1983), pp. 46-47.

6. Bahro, *The Alternative in Eastern Europe*, p. 30.

7. Milovan Djilas, *The New Class: An Analysis of the Communist System* (New York: Frederick A. Praeger, Publisher, 1957), p. 85. In a recent interview Djilas remarked, "What is and what is not socialism is not so clear to me today as when I was young." *New York Times*, June 20, 1982.

8. Marx, *Capital* Volume 1 (New York: International Publishers, 1974): see Chapter 14, Section 5 and Chapter 15, Section 1, especially p. 138. Engels, *Herr Duehring's Revolution in Science [Anti-Duehring]* (New York: International Publishers, 1976), pp. 320-323. Finally, in the *Grundrisse* Marx said, "The principle of developed capital is precisely to make special skill superfluous, and to make manual work, directly physical labor, generally superfluous both as skill and as muscular exertion; to transfer skill, rather, into the dead forces of nature." Translated and introduced by Martin Nicolaus (New York: Vintage Books, 1973), p. 587.

9. This and other examples of the transformation of 'white-collar' jobs are given by Harry Braverman, *Labor and Monopoly Capital* (New York: Monthly Review Press, 1974), passim. Braverman argues very persuasively that the training period of most contemporary jobs are nothing compared to apprenticeship requirements of earlier ages.

10. Marx, *Capital* Volume 3 (New York: International Publishers, 1974), p. 820.

11. Z. A. Jordan in his introduction to *Karl Marx: Economy, Class, and Social Revolution*, edited by Jordan (London: Thomas Nelson and Sons, Ltd., 1971), pp. 53-54.

12. Marx, *Grundrisse*, p. 712.

13. Ibid., pp. 705-706 and p. 708.

14. Ibid., p. 706.

15. Ibid., p. 708.

16. Ibid., p. 488.

17. Ibid., pp. 611-612.

18. G. W. F. Hegel, *The Phenomenology of Mind*, translated by J. B. Baillie (New York: Harper Torchbooks, 1967), pp. 229-240.

19. Engels described the "leap from the realm of necessity into the realm of freedom" as the transition from capitalism to communism, *not* as an internal division within the communist mode of production: *Anti-Duehring*, p. 310. This is in accord with his acceptance of Hegel's understanding of the relation between freedom and necessity which Engels summed up as "freedom is the appreciation of necessity": ibid., pp. 125-126. Marx, of course, was not unaware of this opinion.

20. As argued in Chapter 4, supra.

194

21. This 'initial choice' is, again, Durkheim's conception in *The Division of Labor in Society* (New York: The Free Press, 1964).

22. Marx and Engels, "The German Ideology," in *Marx-Engels Collected Works* Volume 5 (New York: International Publishers, 1976), pp. 44-45. In the margin Marx wrote, "The first form of ideologists, *priests*, is coincident."

23. Ibid., p. 60.

24. Chapter 5, supra.

25. Harry Braverman, *Labor and Monopoly Capital*, passim.

26. Ibid., pp. 90-91.

27. Philip Corrigan, Harvie Ramsey, and Derek Sayer, "Bolshevism and the U.S.S.R.," *New Left Review* Number 125 (January-February 1981), p. 52.

28. Lenin, "The Immediate Tasks of the Soviet Government" [April 1918], in *Selected Works in Three Volumes* Volume 2 (New York: International Publishers, 1967), pp. 671-675. On 'Taylorism', see ibid., p. 664.

29. Corrigan et al., "Bolshevism," p. 52.

30. Adam Smith, *The Wealth of Nations* [abridged] (New York: The Bobbs-Merrill Co., Inc., 1961), p. 16.

31. Erik Olin Wright, *Class, Crisis, and the State* (London: New Left Books, 1978), p. 38 footnote.

32. Rudolf Bahro, "The Alternative in Eastern Europe," *New Left Review* Number 106 (November-December 1977), pp. 10-12 and passim. See also, Bahro, *The Alternative in Eastern Europe*, passim.

33. Bahro, *The Alternative in Eastern Europe*, pp. 46-47.

34. Wlodzimierz Brus, *Socialist Ownership and Political Systems* (London: Routledge and Kegan Paul, 1975), p. 198.

35. Bahro, *The Alternative*, p. 272.

36. Bertell Ollman, "Marx's Vision of Communism: A Reconstruction," in *Radical Visions of the Future*, edited by Seweryn Bialer (Boulder, CO: Westview Press, 1977), pp. 35-83.

37. Jean-Paul Sartre, *Critique of Dialectical Reason* (London: New Left Books/Verso, 1976). For the most part I have relied on Andre Gorz's outline and analysis: Chapter Seven, "Sartre and Marx," in *Socialism and Revolution* (New York: Anchor Books, 1973), p. 253.

38. Marx, *Value, Price, and Profit* (New York: International Publishers, 1935), p. 57.

39. Bahro, "The Alternative in Eastern Europe," p. 26.

40. Corrigan et al., "Bolshevism," p. 50.

41. Bahro, "The Alternative in Eastern Europe," p. 7.

42. Mihaly Vajda, "The Crisis of the System in Eastern Europe and the Attitude of Hungarian Intellectuals," in *The State and Socialism: Political Essays* (London: Allison and Busby, 1981), p. 126.

43. Vajda, "Is Kadarism an Alternative?," in ibid., p. 137.

44. Brus, *Socialist Ownership and Political Systems*, pp. 208-209.

45. Bahro, *The Alternative in Eastern Europe*, p. 425.

46. Bahro, "The Alternative in Eastern Europe," pp. 10-11.

47. Marx, *Grundrisse*, p. 422 and passim. See also, Engels, *Anti- Duehring*, p. 323.

48. Marx and Engels, "The Manifesto of the Communist Party," in *The Revolutions of 1848: Political Writings Volume I*, edited and introduced by David Fernbach (New York: Random House, 1974), p. 87.

49. Marx, *Capital* Volume 1, pp. 354-356. See also ibid., p. 78.

50. According to Kautsky, ownership of factories by those who worked in them "would mean a change to a new form of capitalism ... The new owners would defend their property, as giving them a privileged position, against laborers seeking work ...": Karl Kautsky, *The Dictatorship of the Proletariat* [1918] (Ann Arbor, MI: University of Michigan Press, 1964), p. 122.

51. Bahro, *The Alternative*, p. 441.

52. Domenico Mario Nuti, "The Contradictions of Socialist Economies: A Marxian Interpretation," in *The Socialist Register 1979*, edited by Ralph Miliband and John Saville (London: Merlin Press, 1979), pp. 259-260 and p. 253.

53. Bahro, "The Alternative in Eastern Europe," pp. 21-25.

54. Karl Kautsky suggested something similar to this: "associations of consumers". In *The Dictatorship of the Proletariat*, p. 123.

55. Interview with Jean-Paul Sartre conducted by *Il Manifesto*, "Masses, Spontaneity, Party," pp. 248-249.

56. Bahro, *The Alternative*, p. 361. See Sartre's phrase, "duality of power": "Masses, Spontaneity, Party," p. 248.

57. Marx and Engels, "The German Ideology," p. 77.

58. Ibid., p. 46. This is why Engels called the oppression of women "the first class oppression": *The Origin of the Family, Private Property, and the State* (New York: International Publishers, 1973), p. 129.

59. Marx, "Conspectus of Bakunin's *Statism and Anarchy*," in *The First International and After: Political Writings Volume III*, edited and introduced by David Fernbach (New York: Random House, 1974), p. 336.

60. Bahro, *The Alternative*, p. 38.

Chapter 11
Every Cook a Statesman?

Marx and Engels seriously underestimated the difficulties of the transition to stateless society. They were primarily misled by their conception of the proletariat as essentially 'self-emancipating', i.e. as a class that does not require autonomous political organization to enable the class to *act* on its class interests. Marx and Engels believed that the proletariat, because of its particular position in the productive process, is more or less *automatically* forged into a class subject. Since the proletariat does not need autonomous political organization in the struggle for its liberation, it is clear that it can immediately dispense with much of the old apparatus when it is constituted as the ruling class.

This is Marx's greatest single theoretical error. As Bahro succinctly noted, "the industrial proletariat as such has not attained the perspectives predicted of it." The working class is not capable of self-emancipation for two reasons. First, as a 'class' in Marx's own definition, as opposed to an 'Estate', the proletariat is partly defined by the fragmentation it suffers because of its existence in exchange society. Consequently, it must be conceptualized by its position in the sphere of circulation as well as by its position in the sphere of production.

When the limited communities of feudalism were replaced by the juridical establishment of independent commodity-owners, social production had to be mediated by the market. These independent commodity-owners necessarily compete with one another. In the case of the proletariat, individuals compete in selling their labor-power, for skilled positions, for housing, and for a variety of consumer goods. This internal competition can only be partly alleviated by the development of labor unions. The creation of labor unions generally only displaces the internal competition of the proletariat, transforming it into a competition between labor unions for jobs and public assistance or, most frequently, a competition between different national proletariats, each demanding protection by its government. Needless to say, this internal competition of the proletariat provides the most fertile ground for its manipulation by anti-socialist forces.

Secondly, the proletariat is also fragmented by its position in the sphere of production itself. The division of labor in the workshop entails different positions in production, each with its own limited interests, outlook, and conception of the whole. This fragmentation is exacerbated by exchange relations but is analytically separate from them. For this reason the abolition of exchange is not sufficient. The forced division of labor itself must be abolished, as Marx so frequently and eloquently argued.

We must clearly acknowledge the proletariat's existence under capitalism if we are to correctly evaluate its possibilities for self-emancipation. This existence is, in Marx's words,

> man in his uncultivated, unsocial aspect, man in his contingent existence, man just as he is, man as he has been corrupted, lost to himself, sold, and exposed to the rule of inhuman conditions and elements by the entire organization of society ...[1]

The proletariat can no more escape these conditions than can the bourgeoisie or peasantry. Therefore, like the bourgeoisie and peasantry, the fragmentation of the proletariat engenders autonomous political organizations which struggle for its liberation. The proletariat must be represented.

There is a second problem with the theory of the transcendence of the state that has also emerged from our discussion. In Marx and Engels' theory, the state is transcended with the development of a central coordinating body that does not stand in a 'representative' relation to society, i.e. a relation of autonomy and command to the rest of society. The autonomy of the coordinating institution varies with the unity of society, therefore the possibility of the central coordinating institution forming 'just another branch of the division of labor' depends on the establishment of community on a society-wide basis. This is unlikely even under communism.

The only apparently available basis of community in a socialized economy is the productive unit. Although the individual productive units can be internally structured such that the fragmenting effects of the division of labor are eliminated, the need for a consensus on macroeconomic policy for the *nation as a whole* resurrects the autonomy of the central body. In order for the central body to perform its unifying function it must have autonomy from the individual productive units. Therefore the original vision of Marx and Engels is much more problematic than they believed.

However the theory of the transcendence of the state need not be rejected out of hand because the transformations of production that *are* possible promise to greatly reduce the representative character of the coordinating body. Socialist society can reduce representation by (1) 'deprivatizing' production, i.e. making the structure of production subject to public deliberation and control, (2) eliminating the fragmentation and competition of individuals resulting from exchange relations, and (3) destroying the fragmentation, ignorance, and powerlessness of individuals which are a consequence of the forced division of labor.

In an early work (1850) Marx briefly stated the necessary program for the establishment of communism:

> socialism is the *declaration of the permanence of the revolution*, the *class dictatorship* of the proletariat as a necessary intermediate point on the path towards the *abolition of class differences in general*, the abolition of all relations of production on which they are based, the abolition of all social relations which correspond to these relations of production, and the revolutionizing of all ideas which stem from these social relations.[2]

Although many of the complexities of the process were only revealed in the actual historical development of socialism, this program is still the only one that does justice to Marx's vision and it is identical to the transcendence of the state. The abolition of the division of labor is central to, and even the *meaning* of, "the abolition of all relations of production" on which classes are based. The major task of socialism is also still the construction of a transitional regime which can initiate this process.

With the abolition of the division of labor and the concomitant development of mass participation in production decisions, the necessity for a "moment of autonomy" can be circumscribed but not eliminated. For this reason, democratization of the center retains the importance that is asserted for it in Eastern European critiques of existing socialism. Neither the abolition of the division of labor nor democratization *alone* is sufficient for the transcendence of the state. However, if they are pursued *together*, I believe that the representative character of the center can be reduced to the extent that it is justifiable to speak of the transcendence of the state.

Marx always hoped to establish a society under modern conditions in which "passive suffrage" would be a reality, a society whose members would be the equal of the ancient Germans in "their democratic instinct which in everything of public concern felt itself concerned."[3] Many will no doubt consider this an unrealistic goal in modern society. It is precisely here that the method of Marx may be more persuasive than the actual arguments he produced. Marx insisted, rightfully, that 'society' and 'politics' are parts of a dialectical whole, that social and political structures mutually condition each other. It follows that a different social form will entail a different political structure, a different structure of 'individuality', even a different motivational structure. Charges of utopianism can always be answered by charges of poverty of imagination and an underdeveloped sense of history. If the twentieth century has taught anything, it is that for better or worse, all things are possible. There is no escape from responsibility.

This does not mean that simply repeating Marx is in any way sufficient. The gravest weakness of Marx's thought and that of his disciples is an inadequate exploration of the importance of the mediation of political institutions. Marxian theory must take an explicitly political turn in order to appropriate the insights of traditional political theory. There are a few in the Marxian tradition whose investigations into alternative political structures have been insufficiently appreciated, for example Jean-Paul Sartre and G. D. H. Cole. There a few others who have attempted to explicate the manner in which political judgment, that elusive but essential concept, is institutionally and historically mediated.[4] If these works and others like them can be integrated into Marxian theory, then revolutionary political theory has just begun.

One thing is certain: we cannot continue as we have. Political change will come; if we are to survive it, we must unlock our political imagination.

1. Marx, "On the Jewish Question," in *Karl Marx: Early Writings*, introduced by Lucio Colletti (New York: Vintage Books, 1975), p. 225.

2. Marx, "The Class Struggles in France: 1848 to 1850," in *Surveys From Exile: Political Writings Volume II*, edited and introduced by David Fernbach (New York: Random House, 1974), p. 123.

3. Engels, *The Origin of the Family, Private Property, and the State* (New York: International Publishers, 1973), p. 215. This work was, as Engels acknowledged, produced by culling the ethnological notebooks of Marx after Marx's death. See Lawrence Krader's edition of the original notebooks of Marx, listed in the bibliography.

4. I have in mind the works of Hannah Arendt and also a book by Ronald Beiner on political judgment.

Bibliography

I. Works by Marx and Engels

Marx, Karl. *Capital* Volumes 1-3. New York: International Publishers, 1974.

_____. *A Contribution to the Critique of Political Economy*. New York: International Publishers, 1970.

_____. *The Ethnological Notebooks of Karl Marx*. Edited and introduced by Lawrence Krader. Assen, the Netherlands: van Gorcum and Comp. B.V., 1974.

_____. *Grundrisse*. Translated and introduced by Martin Nicolaus. New York: Vintage Books, 1973.

_____. *Karl Marx: Early Writings*. Introduced by Lucio Colletti. New York: Vintage Books, 1975.

_____. *The Poverty of Philosophy*. New York: International Publishers, 1973.

_____. *The Revolutions of 1848: Political Writings Volume I*. Edited and introduced by David Fernbach. New York: Random House, 1974.

_____. *Surveys From Exile: Political Writings Volume II*. Edited and introduced by David Fernbach. New York: Random House, 1974.

_____. *The First International and After: Political Writings Volume III*. Edited and introduced by David Fernbach. New York: Random House, 1974.

_____. *Value, Price, and Profit*. New York: International Publishers, 1935.

_____. *Wage-Labor and Capital*. New York: International Publishers, 1976.

Marx, Karl, and Engels, Frederick. *The Holy Family, or Critique of Critical Criticism*. Moscow: Progress Publishers, 1975.

_____. *Marx-Engels Collected Works* Volume 3. New York: International Publishers, 1975.

_____. *Marx-Engels Collected Works* Volume 5. New York: International Publishers, 1976.

_____. *Marx-Engels Collected Works* Volume 10. New York: International Publishers, 1978.

_____. *The Marx-Engels Reader*. Edited by Robert C. Tucker. New York: W. W. Norton and Co., Inc., 1978.

_____. *Marx-Engels Selected Correspondence*. Moscow: Progress Publishers, 1975.

_____. *Writings on the Paris Commune (Marx and Engels)*. Edited and introduced by Hal Draper. New York: Monthly Review Press, 1971.

Engels, Frederick. *Herr Eugen Duehring's Revolution in Science [Anti-Duehring]*. New York: International Publishers, 1976.

_____. *Ludwig Feuerbach and the Outcome of Classical German Philosophy*. New York: International Publishers, 1941.

_____. *The Origin of the Family, Private Property, and the State*. New York: International Publishers, 1973.

_____. *Socialism: Utopian and Scientific*. Moscow: Progress Publishers, 1970.

II. Selected Works of Others

Adamiak, Richard. "The 'Withering Away of the State': A Reconsideration." *The Journal of Politics* Volume 32, Number 1 (February 1970): pp. 3-18.

Althusser, Louis. *For Marx*. New York: Vintage Books, 1970.

_____. *Lenin and Philosophy and Other Essays*. New York: Monthly Review Press, 1971.

Anderson, Perry. "The Antinomies of Antonio Gramsci." *New Left Review* Number 100 (November 1976-January 1977): pp. 5-78.

Anweiler, Oscar. *The Soviets: The Russian Workers', Peasants', and Soldiers' Councils 1905-1921*. New York: Pantheon Books, 1974.

Archer, Peter. *Communism and the Law*. Chester Springs, PA: Dufour Editions, 1963.

Arendt, Hannah. *On Revolution*. New York: Viking Press, 1965.

Averitt, Robert T. *The Dual Economy*. New York: W. W. Norton and Co., Inc., 1968.

Avineri, Shlomo. *Hegel's Theory of the Modern State*. London: Cambridge University Press, 1974.

_____. "How to Save Marx from the Alchemists of Revolution." *Political Theory* Volume 4, Number 1 (February 1976): pp. 35-44.

_____. "Marx's Vision of Future Society." *Dissent* (Summer 1973): pp. 323-331.

_____. *The Social and Political Thought of Karl Marx*. London: Cambridge University Press, 1968.

Bahro, Rudolf. *The Alternative in Eastern Europe.* London: New Left Books/Verso, 1978.

_____. "The Alternative in Eastern Europe." *New Left Review* Number 106 (November-December 1977): pp. 3-37.

Balibar, Etienne. *On the Dictatorship of the Proletariat.* London: New Left Books, 1977.

Berlin, Isaiah. *Four Essays on Liberty.* New York: Oxford University Press, 1969.

Blackburn, Robin, editor. *Revolution and Class Struggle: A Reader in Marxist Politics.* Glascow: Fontana and Collins, 1977.

Block, Fred. "Beyond Relative Autonomy: State Managers as Historical Subjects." *The Socialist Register 1980,* edited by Ralph Miliband and John Saville: pp. 227-242. London: Merlin Press, 1980.

_____. "The Ruling Class Does Not Rule: Notes on the Marxist Theory of the State." *Socialist Review* Number 33 (May-June 1977).

Bobbio, Norberto. "Are There Alternatives to Representative Democracy?" *Telos* Number 35 (Spring 1978): pp. 17-30.

Bober, M. M. *Karl Marx's Interpretation of History.* Cambridge: Harvard University Press, 1950.

Boron, Atilio. "Latin America: Between Hobbes and Friedman." *New Left Review* Number 130 (November-December 1981): pp. 45-66.

Braverman, Harry. *Labor and Monopoly Capital.* New York: Monthly Review Press, 1974.

Bridges, Amy Beth. "Nicos Poulantzas and the Marxist Theory of the State." *Politics and Society* Volume 4, Number 2 (Winter 1974): pp. 161-190.

Brinkley, George A. "The 'Withering' of the State Under Khrushchev." In *Marxism*, edited by Michael Curtis: pp. 315-325. New York: Atherton Press, 1970.

Brus, Wlodzimierz. *The Economics and Politics of Socialism: Collected Essays*. London: Routledge and Kegan Paul, 1973.

_____. *Socialist Ownership and Political Systems*. London: Routledge and Kegan Paul, 1975.

Buber, Martin. *Paths in Utopia*. Boston: Beacon Press, 1949.

Bukharin, Nikolai. *Historical Materialism*. Ann Arbor, MI: University of Michigan Press, 1969.

_____, and Preobrazhensky, E. *The ABC of Communism: An Introduction*. Ann Arbor, MI: University of Michigan Press, 1966.

Carew-Hunt, R. N. *The Theory and Practice of Communism: An Introduction*. New York: MacMillan Co., 1951.

Carrillo, Santiago. *Eurocommunism and the State*. Westport, CN: Lawrence Hill and Co., 1978.

Chiodi, Pietro. *Sartre and Marxism*. Great Britain: Harvester Press, 1976.

Cole, G. D. H. *A History of Socialist Thought*. Volume 1: *The Forerunners, 1789-1850*. London: MacMillan and Co., Ltd., 1955.

_____. *A History of Socialist Thought*. Volume 2: *Marxism and Anarchism, 1850-1890*. London: MacMillan and Co., Ltd., 1954.

_____. *The Meaning of Marxism*. Ann Arbor, MI: University of Michigan Press, 1966.

Colletti, Lucio. *From Rousseau to Lenin: Studies in Ideology and Society*. New York: Monthly Review Press, 1972.

210

_____. Introduction to *Karl Marx: Early Writings*: pp. 7-56. New York: Vintage Books, 1975.

"Lucio Colletti: A Political and Philosophical Interview." Interviewed by Perry Anderson. In *Western Marxism: A Critical Reader*: pp. 315-350. London: New Left Books, 1977.

Connolly, William E. "A Note on Freedom Under Socialism." *Political Theory* Volume 5, Number 4 (November 1977): pp. 461-472.

Cornforth, Maurice. *Historical Materialism*. New York: International Publishers, 1971.

Cornu, Auguste. *The Origins of Marxian Thought*. Springfield, IL: Charles C. Thomas, Publisher, 1957.

Corrigan, Philip; Ramsey, Harvie; and Sayer, Derek. "Bolshevism and the U.S.S.R." *New Left Review* Number 125 (January-February 1981): pp. 45-60.

_____. *Socialist Construction and Marxist Theory*. New York: Monthly Review Press, 1978.

DeGeorge, Richard T. *The New Marxism*. New York: Western Publishing Co., Inc., 1968.

della Volpe, Galvano. *Rousseau and Marx and Other Writings*. Atlantic Highlands, NJ: Humanities Press, 1979.

Djilas, Milovan. *The New Class: An Analysis of the Communist System*. New York: Frederick A. Praeger, Publisher, 1957.

_____. *The Unperfect Society: Beyond the New Class*. New York: Harcourt, Brace, and World, Inc., 1969.

_____. "Interview: Yugoslavia's Milovan Djilas." *The New York Times*, June 20, 1982.

Dolgoff, Sam, editor. *Bakunin on Anarchy*. New York: Alfred A. Knopf, 1972.

Draper, Hal. "The Death of the State in Marx and Engels." *The Socialist Register 1970*, edited by Ralph Miliband and John Saville: pp. 281-307. London: Merlin Press, 1970.

_____. "The Dictatorship of the Proletariat." In *Marxism*, edited by Michael Curtis: pp. 285-296. New York: Atherton Press, 1970.

_____. *Karl Marx's Theory of Revolution*. Volume I, Book 1: *State and Bureaucracy*. New York: Monthly Review Press, 1977.

_____. *Karl Marx's Theory of Revolution*. Volume I, Book 2: *State and Bureaucracy*. New York: Monthly Review Press, 1977.

_____. *Karl Marx's Theory of Revolution*. Volume II: *The Politics of Social Classes*. New York: Monthly Review Press, 1978.

_____. "The Principle of Self-Emancipation in Marx and Engels." *The Socialist Register 1971*, edited by Ralph Miliband and John Saville: pp. 81-109. London: Merlin Press, 1971.

Dupre, Louis. *The Philosophical Foundations of Marxism*. New York: Harcourt, Brace, and World, Inc., 1966.

Durkheim, Emile. *The Division of Labor in Society*. New York: The Free Press, 1964.

_____. *Socialism and Saint-Simon*. Edited and introduced by Alvin Gouldner. Yellow Springs, OH: The Antioch Press, 1958.

Evans, Michael. "Marx Studies." *Political Studies* Volume XVIII, Number 4 (December 1970): pp. 528-535.

Feldberg, Rosalyn L.; Kafatou, Sarah; Taylor, Rosemary; and Wood, Robert. "Self-Management, Democracy, Socialism." *Socialist Review* Number 56 (March-April 1981): pp. 137-152.

Fetscher, Iring. "Marx, Engels, and the Future Society." *Survey* Number 38 (October 1961): pp. 100-110.

Garaudy, Roger. *The Alternative Future: A Vision of Christian Marxism.* New York: Simon and Schuster, 1974.

_____. *The Crisis of Communism.* New York: Grove Press, Inc., 1970.

Gerth, H. H., and Mills, C. Wright, editors. *From Max Weber: Essays in Sociology.* New York: Oxford University Press/Galaxy, 1958.

Giddens, Anthony. *The Class Structure of the Advanced Societies.* New York: Harper Torchbooks, 1975.

Gilbert, Alan. "Salvaging Marx From Avineri." *Political Theory* Volume 4, Number 1 (February 1976): pp. 9-34.

Gorz, Andre. *Socialism and Revolution.* Garden City, NJ: Anchor Books, 1973.

Gramsci, Antonio. *Selections From Political Writings 1910-1920.* Selected and edited by Quintin Hoare. New York: International Publishers, 1977.

_____. *Selections From the Prison Notebooks.* Edited and translated by Quintin Hoare and Geoffrey Nowell Smith. New York: International Publishers, 1971.

Harris, Laurence. "The State and the Economy: Some Theoretical Problems." *The Socialist Register 1980*, edited by Ralph Miliband and John Saville: pp. 243-262. London: Merlin Press, 1980.

Hazard, John N. *Communists and Their Law.* Chicago: University of Chicago Press, 1969.

_____. Introduction to *Soviet Legal Philosophy*. Cambridge: Harvard University Press, 1951.

_____. "The Withering Away of the State: The Function of Law." *Survey* Number 38 (October 1961): pp. 72-79.

Hegedus, Andras; Heller, Agnes; Markus, Maria; and Vajda, Mihaly. *The Humanisation of Socialism: Writings of the Budapest School*. New York: St. Martin's Press, 1976.

Hegel, G. W. F. *The Phenomenology of Mind*. Translated by J. B. Baillie. New York: Harper Torchbooks, 1967.

Hegel's Philosophy of Right. Translated with notes by T. M. Knox. New York: Oxford University Press, 1967.

Hoover, Calvin B. "The Soviet State Fails to Wither." In *Marxism*, edited by Michael Curtis: pp. 305-314. New York: Atherton Press, 1970.

Howard, Dick, editor. *Selected Political Writings: Rosa Luxemburg*. New York: Monthly Review Press, 1971.

Hyman, Richard. "Workers' Control and Revolutionary Theory." *The Socialist Register 1974*, edited by Ralph Miliband and John Saville: pp. 241-278. London: Merlin Press, 1974.

Ionescu, Ghita, editor. *The Political Thought of Saint-Simon*. Introduced by Ghita Ionescu. London: Oxford University Press, 1976.

Jordan, Z. A., editor. Introduction to *Karl Marx: Economy, Class, and Social Revolution*: pp. 9-67. London: Thomas Nelson and Sons, Ltd., 1971.

Kain, Philip J. "Estrangement and the Dictatorship of the Proletariat." *Political Theory* Volume 7, Number 4 (November 1979): pp. 509-520.

Kautsky, Karl. *The Dictatorship of the Proletariat*. Ann Arbor, MI: University of Michigan Press, 1964.

214

_____. *The Labor Revolution*. London: George Allan and Unwin, Ltd., 1925.

_____. *Terrorism and Communism*. Westport, CN: Hyperion Press, Inc., 1973.

Kellner, Douglas, editor. *Karl Korsch: Revolutionary Theory*. Austin, TX: University of Texas Press, 1977.

Kline, George. "The Withering Away of the State: Philosophy and Practice." *Survey* Number 38 (October 1961): pp. 63-71.

Korsch, Karl. *Three Essays on Marxism*. New York: Monthly Review Press, 1972.

Labedz, Leopold. "The New C.P.S.U. Programme: Ideology and Utopia." *Survey* Number 38 (October 1961): pp. 12-28.

Laclau, Ernesto. *Politics and Ideology in Marxist Theory*. Atlantic Highlands, NJ: Humanities Press, 1977.

Laqueur, Walter Z. "Introduction." *Survey* Number 38 (October 1961): pp. 3-11.

Laski, Harold J. *Communism*. New York: Henry Holt and Co., 1927.

Lefebvre, Henri. *The Sociology of Marx*. New York: Vintage Books, 1969.

Lenin, V. I. *Selected Works in Three Volumes* Volumes 1-3. New York: International Publishers, 1967.

Lichtheim, George. *Georg Lukacs*. New York: Viking Press, 1970.

_____. *Marxism: An Historical and Critical Study*. New York: Praeger Publishers, 1965.

Lukacs, Georg. *History and Class Consciousness.* Cambridge: The MIT Press, 1971.

_____. *Lenin: A Study on the Unity of His Thought.* Cambridge: The MIT Press, 1971.

_____. *Tactics and Ethics: Political Essays, 1919-1929.* New York: Harper and Row, Publishers, 1972.

McGovern, Arthur F., S.J. "The Young Marx on the State." *Science and Society* Volume 34, Number 4 (Fall 1970): pp. 430-466.

McClellan, David. *Marxism After Marx.* New York: Harper and Row, Publishers, 1979.

_____. *Marx Before Marxism.* New York: Harper and Row, Publishers, 1970.

_____. "Marx's View of the Unalienated Society." *The Review of Politics* Volume 31, Number 4 (October 1969): pp. 459-465.

_____. *The Thought of Karl Marx: An Introduction.* London: Mac-Millan Press, Ltd., 1972.

McMurtry, John. *The Structure of Marx's World-View.* Princeton: Princeton University Press, 1978.

Mandel, Ernest. *From Stalinism to Eurocommunism.* London: New Left Books, 1978.

_____. *Marxist Economic Theory.* Two Volumes. New York: Monthly Review Press, 1968.

_____. "A Political Interview." *New Left Review* Number 100 (November 1976-January 1977): pp. 97-132.

216

Marcuse, Herbert. "Protosocialism and Late Capitalism: Toward a Theoretical Synthesis Based on Bahro's Analysis." In *Rudolf Bahro: Critical Responses*, edited by Ulf Wolter: pp. 25-48. White Plains, NY: M. E. Sharpe, 1980.

Markham, F. M. H., editor. *Henri Comte de Saint-Simon: Selected Writings*. Oxford: Basil Blackwell, 1952.

Mattick, Paul. *Anti-Bolshevik Communism*. White Plains, NY: M. E. Sharpe, 1978.

Mayo, Henry B. *Introduction to Marxist Theory*. London: Oxford University Press, 1960.

Merleau-Ponty, Maurice. *Adventures of the Dialectic*. Evanston, IL: Northwestern University Press, 1973.

Meszaros, Istvan. *Marx's Theory of Alienation*. London: Merlin Press, 1970.

_____. "Political Power and Dissent in Post-Revolutionary Societies." *New Left Review* Number 108 (March-April 1978): pp. 3-21.

Meyer, Alfred G. *Communism*. New York: Random House, 1967.

Miliband, Ralph. "A Commentary on Bahro's Alternative." *The Socialist Register 1979*, edited by Ralph Miliband and John Saville: pp. 274-284. London: Merlin Press, 1965.

_____. "Marx and the State." *The Socialist Register 1965*, edited by Ralph Miliband and John Saville: pp. 278-296. London: Merlin Press, 1965.

_____. *Marxism and Politics*. Oxford: Oxford University Press, 1977.

Miller, David. "Socialism and the Market." *Political Theory* Volume 5, Number 4 (November 1977): pp. 473-490.

218

Pelczynski, Z. A., editor. *Hegel's Political Philosophy: Problems and Perspectives.* London: Cambridge University Press, 1971.

Pennock, J. Roland, and Chapman, John W., editors. *Representation* (Nomos X). New York: Atherton Press, 1968.

Pitkin, Hannah. *The Concept of Representation.* Berkeley: University of California Press, 1967.

_____, editor. *Representation.* New York: Atherton Press, 1969.

Plamenatz, John. *Man and Society* Volume II. New York: McGraw-Hill Book Co., Inc., 1963.

Plekhanov, George V. *Fundamental Problems of Marxism.* New York: International Publishers, 1969.

Popper, Karl. *The Open Society and Its Enemies.* Volume II: *Hegel and Marx.* Princeton: Princeton University Press, 1971.

Poulantzas, Nicos. *Fascism and Dictatorship.* London: New Left Books, 1974.

_____. *Political Power and Social Classes.* London: New Left Books, 1973.

_____. "Political Parties and the Crisis of Marxism.: Interview by Stuart Hill and Alan Hunt. *Socialist Review* Number 48 (November-December 1979): pp. 57-74.

_____. "The State and the Transition to Socialism." Interview by Henri Weber. *Socialist Review* Number 38 (March-April 1978): pp. 9-36.

_____. *State, Power, Socialism.* London: New Left Books/Verso, 1978.

Przeworski, Adam. "Proletariat into Class: The Process of Class Formation from Karl Kautsky's *The Class Struggle* to Recent Controversies." *Politics and Society* Volume 7, Number 4 (Summer 1977): pp. 343-401.

Radice, Lucio Lombardo. "State Socialism." In *Rudolf Bahro: Critical Responses*, edited by Ulf Wolter: pp. 129-151. White Plains, NY: M. E. Sharpe, Inc., 1980.

Ramm, Thilo. "The Utopian Tradition." *Survey* Number 38 (October 1961): pp. 91-99.

Rossanda, Rossana. "Class and Party." *The Socialist Register 1970*, edited by Ralph Miliband and John Saville: pp. 217-231. London: Merlin Press, 1970.

Rubel, Maximilien. "Notes on Marx's Conception of Democracy." *New Politics* Winter 1962: pp. 78-90.

Sartre, Jean-Paul. *The Communists and Peace.* New York: George Braziller, Inc., 1968.

_____. *Critique of Dialectical Reason.* London: New Left Books/Verso, 1976.

_____. "Masses, Spontaneity, Party." Interview by *Il Manifesto. The Socialist Register 1970*, edited by Ralph Miliband and John Saville: pp. 233-249. London: Merlin Press, 1970.

Schaff, Adam. *Marxism and the Human Individual.* New York: McGraw-Hill Book Co., 1970.

Schwartz, Nancy. "Distinction Between Public and Private Life: Marx on the *zoon politikon.*" *Political Theory* Volume 7, Number 2 (May 1979): pp. 245-266.

Selucky, R. "Marxism and Self-Management." In *Self-Management: Economic Liberation of Man*, edited by Jaroslav Vanek: pp. 47-61. Baltimore: Penguin Education, 1975.

Stalin, Josif. "Anarchism or Socialism." in *Stalin: Works* Volume I: pp. 297-319. Moscow: Foreign Languages Publishing House, 1952.

_____. "Report to the XVIII Party Congress." In *Soviet Legal Philosophy*, introduced by John N. Hazard: pp. 343-349. Cambridge: Harvard University Press, 1951.

Talmon, J. L. *The Origins of Totalitarian Democracy*. New York: Frederick A. Praeger, Publishers, 1960.

Tarschys, Daniel. *Beyond the State: The Future Polity in Classical and Soviet Marxism*. n.p. Scandinavian University Books, 1971.

Therborn, Goran. "The Rule of Capital and the Rise of Democracy." *New Left Review* Number 103 (May-June 1977): pp. 3-41.

_____. *What Does the Ruling Class Do When It Rules?* London: New Left Books, 1978.

Thomas, Paul. *Karl Marx and the Anarchists*. London: Routledge and Kegan Paul, 1980.

Tillich, Paul. *The Socialist Decision*. New York: Harper and Row, Publishers, 1977.

Triska, Jan F., editor. *Constitutions of the Communist Party-States*. n.p. Hoover Institution Publications, 1968.

Tucker, Robert C. "Marx as a Political Theorist." In *Marx and the Western World*, edited by Nicolaus Lobkowicz: pp. 103-131. South Bend, IN: University of Notre Dame Press, 1967.

221

_____. *The Marxian Revolutionary Idea*. New York: W. W. Norton and Co., Inc., 1970.

_____. *Philosophy and Myth in Karl Marx*. London: Cambridge University Press, 1972.

Vajda, Mihaly. *The State and Socialism: Political Essays*. London: Allison and Busby, 1981.

Vitak, Robert. "Workers' Control: The Czechoslovak Experience." *The Socialist Register 1971*, edited by Ralph Miliband and John Saville: pp. 245-264. London: Merlin Press, 1971.

Voegelin, Eric. "The Formation of the Marxian Revolutionary Idea." *The Review of Politics* Volume 12, Number 3 (July 1950): pp. 275-302.

Vuskovic, Boris. "Social Inequality in Yugoslavia." *New Left Review* Number 95 (January-February 1976): pp. 26-44.

Vyshinsky, A. Y. "The Soviet State in the War for the Fatherland." In *Soviet Legal Philosophy*, introduced by John N. Hazard: pp. 427-432. Cambridge: Harvard University Press, 1951.

Waters, Mary Alice, editor. *Rosa Luxemburg Speaks*. New York: Pathfinder Press, 1970.

Wolfe, Alan. "New Directions in the Marxist Theory of Politics." *Politics and Society* Volume 4, Number 2 (Winter 1974): pp. 131-159.

Wolfe, Bertram D. *Marxism: One Hundred Years in the Life of a Doctrine*. New York: Dial Press, 1965.

Wright, Erik Olin. *Class, Crisis, and the State*. London: New Left Books, 1978.

Zauberman, Alfred. "Value, Price, and Profit." *Survey* Number 38 (October 1961): pp. 54-62.

Index of Names

Douglas Beck Low

THE EXISTENTIAL DIALECTIC OF MARX AND MERLEAU-PONTY

American University Studies: Series V (Philosophy). Vol. 33
ISBN 0-8204-0435-7   260 pages   hardback US $ 36.00 / sFr. 54.00

Recommended prices – alterations reserved

The Existential Dialectic of Marx and Merleau-Ponty is one of the few books to offer an in depth epistemological study linking the works of Karl Marx with a major existentialist thinker. The author first documents the existential and dialectical themes that can be found in Marx's writings and then proceeds to show that Marx's method is strikingly similar to that employed by Merleau-Ponty. It is Merleau-Ponty, however, who has developed this method in detail. Dr. Low thus turns to a thorough analysis and exposition of Merleau-Ponty's first major work, *The Structure of Behavior,* to reveal Merleau-Ponty's innovative and well-balanced alternative to traditional empiricism and rationalism. Merleau-Ponty's method, as it is revealed here, will be of interest to philosophers, psychologists and social scientists concerned with freeing themselves from the limitations imposed by traditional methodologies.

Contents: *The Existential Dialectic of Marx and Douglas Low* offers the reader a probing study of the respective methodologies of Marx and Merleau-Ponty – This comparative study has led the author to detailed analysis and exposition of Merleau-Ponty's often ignored early work, *The Structure of Behavior.*

«*This unique volume creatively relates Merleau-Ponty's dialectical methodology and epistemology to the dialectical methodology and humanism of Karl Marx. Thereby the author counters more scientific and reductionistic interpretations of contemporary philosophy including such an interpretation of Marx.*» (Harold A. Durfee, William Frazer McDowell, Professor of Philosophy, The American University)

PETER LANG PUBLISHING, INC.
62 West 45th Street
USA – New York, NY 10036

Joel Tabora

THE FUTURE IN THE WRITINGS OF KARL MARX
An Evaluative Interpretation Based on Primary Sources

European University Studies: Series XX (Philosophy). Vol. 131
ISBN 0-8204-7977-5   435 pages   paperback sFr. 78.00

Recommended price – alterations reserved

It was in critical humanistic intent that Marx attempted the overturning of Hegel's dialectic in Historical Materialism: understanding future human humanity as the necessary overcoming («Aufhebung») of private productivity which fails to satisfy man's human need. This study, based on a spectrum of primary sources from the young to the mature Marx, presents the critical function and the praxis-inductive role the future had in Marx's thought. The promise that continues to live in this thought is thereby explicated. It is however a promise premised on a persistent idealism in Marx's claimed materialism which compromises the depth of man's human need in a future whose realization is necessarily (only) future.

Contents: Future in Marxian materialism: as result of Marx's critique of Hegelian dialectic – As the transcendence of private property («Economic and philosophic manuscripts») – As the negation of human negation in the commodity fetish («Capital»).

PETER LANG PUBLISHING, INC.
62 West 45th Street
USA – New York, NY 10036